Religious bibliographies in serial literature: a guide

Religious bibliographies in serial literature: a guide

Compiled by
Michael J. Walsh
with the help of
John V. Howard
Graham P. Cornish
Robert J. Duckett
on behalf of
the Association of British Theological
and Philosophical Libraries

Greenwood Press
Westport, Connecticut

Published in the United States and Canada by Greenwood
Press, a division of Congressional Information Service, Inc.,
Westport, Connecticut

English language edition, except the United States and
Canada, published by Mansell Publishing, a member of
Bemrose U.K. Limited

First published 1981

Library of Congress Cataloging in Publication Data

Walsh, Michael J
Religious bibliographies in serial literature.

Bibliography: p.
Includes index.
1. Religion – Periodicals – Bibliography.
2. Theology – Periodicals – Bibliography. I. Title.
Z7753.W34 [BL1]   016.200'5   81-312
ISBN 0-313-22987-2   AACR1

Printed in Great Britain

Contents

Foreword

The shock waves of the information explosion have reached the cloisters of theology and religion, and librarians and scholars seek to control the mass of material at their disposal. Transistors and microprocessors are on their way, but, in these subject fields, their effect has hardly been felt as yet.

Meantime, the manual methods of indexing and retrieval hold sway – and to a far greater extent than many realize. Conscious of this, a group of members of ABTAPL (the Association of British Theological and Philosophical Libraries) have produced this *Guide* to existing indexing and abstracting services in the fields served by their various libraries. Many of these services are little known outside their own speciality. The range of subjects is wide, and much experience is available here for sharing.

The project started with a proposal from Michael Walsh at the Canterbury meeting of ABTAPL in May 1977. It was pursued by the compilers in correspondence and in further meetings in London, Boston Spa, and Hawarden. The named compilers are also indebted for substantial contributions from Carole Rogers of Birmingham City Libraries (Philosophy and Religion Department) and Stephen Poole of Heythrop College Library.

It is therefore essentially a cooperative project, and its future must equally depend on cooperation from its users. For no guide that aims to lead the way through the labyrinth of currently published indexes in any field can hope to remain up to date for very long – even if it succeeds in indicating a few dead ends! But there has not been such a guide to the bibliography of these subjects before, and we hope that this thread, so laboriously spun, will be a lifeline to many.

John V. Howard
Chairman, ABTAPL

New College,
Edinburgh

Introduction
The bibliography of religion – a survey

In an article published in 1973 R. J. Duckett, one of the contributors to this *Guide*, drew attention to what he called 'The parlous state of the librarianship of religion'.[1] His criticisms were eminently justified, and the situation has changed little over the last half-dozen years. This *Guide* is an attempt to fill one of the gaps in the bibliography of religion upon which that article commented.

The origins of this book have already been described by John Howard in his Foreword. Its purpose is to put before both librarians and students of religion the vast wealth of bibliographical material which is available to help them keep up to date with the enormous range of books and articles appearing each year within their sphere of interest. It is a belief shared by the compilers of this *Guide* that many who find themselves in charge of theological collections of one sort or another, whether they be in seminary libraries, for example, or in the 'philosophy and religion' departments of large university or public libraries, are unaware of the variety and scale of the resources which are already available for their use. And if librarians are unaware of them, then we suspect that many of those who study and teach religion are at least equally, and perhaps even more, out of touch with a great many of the bibliographical tools already on their library shelves.

No criticism is intended by this of those who find themselves in control of theological collections. Few professional librarians have been trained specifically in the field of religious bibliography, though there is some slight indication that this may be changing. But it was Mr. Duckett's contention, in the article quoted above, that many theological libraries are in the charge of people who have received no professional training, either because the institutions which these libraries serve do not see the value of employing professional staff, or because they cannot afford to do so. Even allowing for the relative size of the populations, and the number of institutions, across the Atlantic and on the other side of the Channel, the number of librarians engaged full time in the librarianship of religion in the United Kingdom is very small indeed compared to the numbers who are members of the American Theological Library Association and similar organizations both in the U.S.A. and on the continent of Europe.[2]

The nearest equivalent of ATLA in these islands is the modest Association of British Theological and Philosophical Libraries (ABTAPL) with well under 100 members, both personal and institutional, in Great Britain and Ireland. It is beneath the auspices of ABTAPL that this *Guide* is produced. The Association 'was founded in 1956 to bring together librarians working with, or interested in, theological literature in Great Britain. Its purposes were to improve the bibliographical information available, to bring to light some of the little known collections on these subjects, and to help the smaller libraries that lacked professional expertise'.[3] Its journal, the ABTAPL *Bulletin*, ceased to appear in 1966, but revived in 1974 under the energetic editorship of the present ABTAPL chairman. Apart from Association news and announcements, the main feature of the *Bulletin* is a 'reference section' which provides information concerning libraries, societies, bibliographies and reference works of interest to librarians of religion. Written largely in non-technical language, it is designed to assist the untrained, and often voluntary staff who run so many of the theological libraries in the United Kingdom.[4]

One of ABTAPL's earliest projects, undertaken with the help of a small grant from the British Library Association, was a *Handbook of Theological Libraries*. Some 250 such libraries were identified, and questionnaires sent out. For reasons beyond the control of ABTAPL, however, this project has not been completed, and there is still no adequate listing of religious libraries in the United Kingdom. For coverage of these one has to have recourse to much more general works, such as the *ASLIB Directory* or *The Libraries, Museums and Art Galleries Year Book*. Both draw attention, through their indexes, to the existence of theological libraries, and to the major theological collections in more general libraries, but neither contains anywhere near the number of entries which Philip Plumb, its editor, envisioned for the ill-fated *Handbook*. It is interesting to see that in the recent *Research Libraries and Collections in the United Kingdom: A Selective Inventory and Guide*, although 247 libraries are included, and the index lists many entries of interest to students of religion, not a single specifically religious library is mentioned by the compiler. One will expect better results from the *Directory of Rare Book Collections* at present being compiled by the Rare Books Group of the Library Association.

The problem for a researcher in religious studies, however, is not simply that he will not know where to find libraries specializing in his field. He will also find it difficult to encounter librarians with some especial knowledge of the subject of his research who will be able to guide him in his bibliographic endeavours. This will remain troublesome until the proposed *Handbook* or something comparable is produced. But in the meantime perhaps it may be worthwhile to draw attention to the existence of just three libraries, New College (University of Edinburgh) in the North of the British Isles, Selly Oak Colleges (Birmingham) in the centre, and Heythrop College (University of London) in the South, which should be able to help with the more complex bibliographical queries beyond the scope of the non-specialist librarian.[5] In addition, two specialist libraries in London will lend by post to their subscribing members, Dr. Williams's Library and the Catholic Central Library.[6] These two conveniently cover the spectrum from Nonconformity to Roman Catholicism.

Students of religion, meanwhile, should remember that the very best collections of theological literature, as of practically any other sort of literature, are likely to be found in the great national libraries. And the British Library Lending Division at Boston Spa, West Yorkshire, which one can approach through one's university or public library, is at least as good a source for theological material as for any other.

Introduction

In addition to the complaint Mr. Duckett voiced in his article about the lack of any single listing of religious collections and libraries, he regretted the absence of a specialist British indexing or abstracting service in the field of religious studies. The one exception he could find was Graham Cornish's *Theological and Religious Index*.[7] This was published between 1971 and 1975, when pressure of work forced its compiler to abandon his project, at least for the time being. Its purpose was to scan journals which would not usually be noticed by theologians for articles of interest to them. It was Mr. Cornish's belief that much valuable material goes unread because it is published in journals peripheral to the general study of religion. Mr. Cornish's thinking has had a considerable influence upon the compilers of this *Guide*, of which number he was one of the most active. When a list of indexing and abstracting services to be included was drawn up, many claimed a place even though, at first sight, it might have seemed they had little or nothing to do with the study of religion. They were considered for inclusion because all had, either as a separate section in the body of the book or in the index, some heading such as 'Religion', 'Theology', 'Islam' and so on. Had all of these bibliographical services been covered, the *Guide* would have become too unwieldy to use. It would have drawn the attention of its users to indexing services which could rarely, if ever, satisfy their needs. It was therefore decided to list only those services which, in addition to having a separate entry with some heading such as those mentioned above, listed within it at least a score of items annually – though exceptions to this general rule have occasionally had to be made. It is a feature of this *Guide* to current bibliographies in religious studies that between obvious entries such as *The Pope Speaks* and *Quaker History* there are to be found *Psychological Abstracts* and *Public Affairs Information Bulletin*.

One of the conclusions to be drawn from the wide scope of the 178 entries in this Guide – and undoubtedly there are many other publications unknown to, or overlooked by, the compilers, which merit inclusion – is that there is no shortage of bibliographies of current literature covering religion in all its many aspects. Indeed, the problem may be the opposite. There may be too many competing ones, and no single exhaustive bibliography in the field which can be recommended without qualification. As far as books are concerned, however, it is well to remember the existence for many countries of the world of national bibliographies. The *British National Bibliography* has been included as an example (for details, see No. 53) but others, particularly the German one given the wealth of theological publication in that country, might equally have been cited. National bibliographies are expensive items, but *BNB* is usually readily available in public and university libraries. It can be searched for books on religion either through its classification system – a not wholly reliable approach – or through the regular subject indexes, and the same may be said for the most part of other national bibliographies.

While *BNB* should keep a researcher reasonably well informed about books on his subject published in England,[8] it cannot help that person to establish retrospective bibliographies. For these the student of religion is well served by the catalogues of major collections, some of which have been published and may be consulted in the larger libraries. There is a subject index to the *British Museum General Catalogue of Printed Books*, but the researcher is well advised to look first at the *Library of Congress Catalog, Books: Subjects*. It is a cumulative list of works represented by Library of Congress printed cards, and is arranged under subjects. To derive full benefit from this, the user really needs access to the Library of Congress list of subject headings, but that, too, should be available in a large library. The *Library of Congress Catalog* is easier to use than its British Library equivalent, and more thorough.[9]

It was the intention of the compilers of this *Guide* to include only those bibliographical tools which appeared, in theory at least, once a year or more frequently. Library catalogues were, therefore, excluded from consideration. There is, however, an annual up-date to the catalogue of Dr. Williams's Library, and that has therefore earned a place (No. 58).

Despite their omission from this *Guide*, it would be a

mistake not to refer to library catalogues when pursuing the bibliography of religion. Even some libraries which might not at first sight seem to have a great deal to do with theology can be extremely useful. A researcher on Church–State relations in practically any country (and therefore in any religious tradition) of the world could scarcely do better than to turn to the *London Bibliography of the Social Sciences*, based on the holdings of the British Library of Political and Economic Science, serving one of the colleges of London University. At the end of each of the volumes the heading Philosophy and Religion encompasses a long list of sub-headings which are of interest to theologians. The School of Oriental and African Studies, also part of London University, produces a bulky *Monthly List of Titles added to the Catalogue*. Though this *Monthly List* rarely includes enough entries under its A 200 classification for religion to qualify it for entry here, no one interested in the religions of Africa, or the Middle and Far East can afford to ignore it.

The library catalogues so far described, apart from that of Dr. Williams's Library, are only marginally concerned with religious subjects. Of those more closely concerned with the topics covered in this *Guide* there is room here to mention only three which may stand as examples for the different kinds available: the *Methodist Union Catalogue: Pre-1976 Imprints*, of which three volumes (up to 'Dixon') have so far appeared; the two-volume *Classified Catalog of the Ecumenical Movement*; and, in four volumes, the *Fichier Augustinien/ Augustine Bibliography*. The first of these is based on the holdings of over 200 libraries, mainly in the United States of America but also elsewhere, and is, therefore, a union list as the title indeed indicates. Locations are given for the items included. The library of the World Council of Churches at Geneva has provided the basis for the second catalogue, though the cards for only those of its holdings dealing specifically with ecumenics, have been reproduced. The *Fichier Augustinien* reproduces the entire card catalogue, some 60,000 entries strong, of the library of the Institut des Études Augustiniennes in Paris, an institute devoted to the study of St. Augustine of Hippo. The *Classified Catalog* and the *Fichier Augustinien* were both published in 1972. An entirely different kind of catalogue is the *Historical Catalogue of the Printed Editions of Holy Scripture in the Library of the British and Foreign Bible Society*. This lists the printed Bibles in the Society's collection in order of the date of their publication, and gives a full bibliographic description of them. It has become such a standard work that it is known to bibliographers simply by the surnames of its two compilers, T. H. Darlow and H. F. Moule. First published in 1903 it was reprinted 60 years later. In 1968, A. S. Herbert published a revision and expansion of the section devoted to Bibles in English.

The examples given in the last few paragraphs may perhaps serve to indicate how wide a field religious bibliography can be. Control of the subject is a nightmare. John G. Barrow attempted to bring some sort of order into it in 1955 with his *Bibliography of Bibliographies in religion*. Useful though this work may still sometimes be despite its age, it cannot be compared for thoroughness to Shlomo Shunami's survey of just one relatively small area in his *Bibliography of Jewish Bibliographies*. The second edition of this work, containing 4750 entries, appeared in 1965. A decade later a supplement took the number of entries up to 6827. These retrospective bibliographies cannot of course be kept up to date except at fairly lengthy intervals. In between times the attention of researchers into religion should be drawn to the *Bibliographic Index* (No. 37). Published for over 30 years it is a quarterly listing, with annual cumulations, of bibliographies which have appeared as independent publications, or as parts of books, pamphlets or periodicals. To qualify for inclusion the bibliography must have over 50 entries.

The *Bibliographic Index* can help to keep the researcher reasonably well up to date with the mass of bibliographical material which appears year by year. But religion deals very largely with the past. Its literature does not date as quickly as, say, works on astrophysics, and the subject appears to induce a bibliographical urge in its practitioners. The number of retrospective bibliographies is enormous, as the compilations of Barrow and Shunami demonstrate. There is, for example, the *Baptist Bibliography* compiled by Edward

C. Starr in 25 massive tomes. Though an index is provided for each it is difficult to see how one could use such a work with any great ease. Religious orders have produced surveys of writings of their members, though few of the Orders can compete with Carlos Sommervogel's *Bibliothèque de la Compagnie de Jesus*, and its regular up-date, the *Index Bibliographicus Societatis Iesu*.[10]

This sort of bibliography exists in abundance for the whole field of religious research. One might draw attention, for example, to H. W. Turner's *Bibliography of New Religious Movements in Primal Societies*. The first volume of nearly 300 pages was devoted to Black Africa, and the second, of a similar size, to North America. Or there is William J. Wainwright's *Philosophy of Religion: An Annotated Bibliography of Twentieth-Century Writings in English* with 1135 entries in nearly 800 pages. This last book was published in London and New York by Garland Publishing Inc., which, under the general heading of Reference Titles in Philosophy and Religion, has produced a number of important bibliographical studies. In addition to Wainwright's volume there are, for example, *A Bibliography of Buddhist Scriptures* compiled by Edward Conze and edited by Lewis Lancaster; or *Pierre Teilhard de Chardin: A Comprehensive Bibliography*, put together by Joseph M. McCarthy. A somewhat similar series was published in the 1970s by the Clifford E. Barbour Library of the Pittsburgh Theological Seminary under the title Bibliographia Tripotamopolitana. The most recent work, No. 11, appeared in 1979: *A Bibliography of Semiological and Structural Studies of Religion*, compiled by Alfred M. Johnson. Earlier publications have included bibliographies of Richard Hooker (No. 4), John Bunyan (No. 5), Zwingli (No. 7), Quincy Wright (No. 8) and five English mystics (No. 10).

Scholars of religion in general need not lack for bibliographies, but within that general field no area appears to be so thoroughly covered as Biblical studies, and in particular the New Testament. A useful, slim and cheap guide to these can be found in R. T. France's *A Bibliographical Guide to New Testament Research*, published by the enterprising JSOT Press based on the Department of Biblical Studies at Sheffield University. In addition to the bibliographies of topics within New Testament studies compiled by Bruce Metzger and others, France lists J. C. Hurd's *Bibliography of New Testament Bibliographies* published in 1966 and St. John's University Library's *Index to Biblical Journals*, a computer-generated index produced in 1971 to some of the more important journals published in the course of the previous half century.

Though New Testament studies may be especially well supplied with bibliographies, almost any topic, no matter how small, is likely to be covered by an entry in an encyclopaedia. And in the better encyclopaedias bibliographies are usually appended to the foot of the entry. The *Encyclopaedia Judaica* was published in 1972 in sixteen volumes. The new edition of the *Encyclopaedia of Islam* began to appear in 1960 and is still under way. The *Dictionnaire de Spiritualité* has so far produced nine volumes and only reached the entry 'Lyonnet' since it began in 1937, while the *Theologische Realenzyklopädie* has got as far as 'Autobiographie' in Volume 4. The five volumes of the *Dizionario degli Istituti di Perfezione*, a work which discusses people and concepts as well as the history of the religious orders and congregations, has taken five volumes and six years to arrive at 'Monachesimo'. The excellent, and too little-known, *Bibliotheca Sanctorum* (written in Italian despite its Latin name) was published in thirteen volumes during the 1960s by the Lateran University in Rome. It may eventually be replaced by the *Biographisch-Bibliographisches Kirchenlexikon* which began to appear under the editorship of F. W. Bautz in 1975, but it will be many years before this mammoth enterprise is complete. All of these encyclopaedias have excellent bibliographies. Of course, even in the case of those still in progress, the bibliographical information contained in parts already published will have become out of date.[11] But it is the purpose of the present *Guide* to show that although retrospective bibliography in religious studies is fairly easy, keeping up to date is easier than may at first sight appear, given the number and variety of indexing and abstracting services available to the researcher.

Much less satisfactory is the provision of news and current awareness services in the religious field. The situation may have improved slightly since Mr. Duckett drew attention to this gap in 1973, but many of his complaints still apply. No library has a complete run of the *Church Times* or the *Catholic Herald*. No library is recorded as holding back numbers of *L'Osservatore Romano*, the Vatican daily newspaper. In the United Kingdom there is nothing similar to Thor Hall's *Directory of Systematic Theologians in North America*, or to J. Gordon Melton's recent *Directory of Religious Bodies in the United States*. A little of this kind of information can be gleaned from such standard works as *The World of Learning* – but not a great deal. More is available from the directories issued by individual Churches in the United Kingdom, *The Church of England Year Book* and the *Catholic Directory* to mention two obvious examples, but it is difficult to extract and, in any case, there are no interdenominational works of reference of this sort. For guidance to the complexities of ecclesiastical hierarchies, researchers on this side of the Atlantic will have to rely upon, and transpose to Great Britain as best they may, the information contained in Arthur Piepkorn's *Profiles in Belief*.

One must draw the conclusion that the state of the librarianship of religion is only marginally less parlous in 1980 than when Mr. Duckett wrote his article on the subject in 1973. Though it appears to flourish in the United States, it struggles in the United Kingdom, despite the extremely valuable holdings of which so many of our ancient theological libraries can boast. The task of librarians of these collections, however, is too often simply the maintenance of existing stock in some state of repair on already meagre and always diminishing funds. They are not in a position to buy for the assistance of their readers even such basic tools as the *Book Review Index* or the new *Arts and Humanities Citation Index*. Items like these are expensive enough for any library, but in large university or public collections they take up a relatively small proportion of the total book fund. They bulk too large to contemplate for small divinity faculty, seminary or private theological libraries. And, one suspects, because they are rarely seen within religious libraries the advantage of them for research purposes is not sufficiently appreciated by students of religion. There is a danger that theologians in the United Kingdom will come to believe, if they do not believe it already, that the poverty of resources in the field of religious bibliography and current awareness is comparable to that suffered by their colleagues in other disciplines. The danger becomes all the greater with the introduction into libraries of modern technology. Unless part of some university scheme, no theological library in the United Kingdom foresees the installation of computer terminals to speed literature searching, or for cataloguing purposes. And though several of the bibliographies listed in this *Guide* are compiled by computer, no specifically religious bibliography is as yet available on line.

The logic is irresistible: a shortage of funds for theological libraries means a shortage of tools produced with their particular needs in mind. And a shortage of such bibliographical tools means, in turn, a decline in the standards of service which theological libraries can provide. If the libraries suffer, then eventually their users suffer, whether they be academics, clergymen, or interested enquirers of any sort. It may be that the only hope for these libraries is to give up their independence and enter cooperative schemes, a solution only possible in a fairly limited geographical area, or to become parts of a university network, as New College has done in Edinburgh and Heythrop has done in London.

Until theological libraries – and theological librarianship – is more adequately funded, then manual rather than computer-based information retrieval systems hold sway, as Mr. Howard remarked in his Foreword. Hence the importance of this *Guide*, which attempts to draw attention to the wide variety of regularly published bibliographies, many of them not of an obviously religious bent, which can be of assistance in literature searching. The compilers are aware that they will have omitted many which fulfill the criteria for inclusion. The criteria are, first, regular, and at least annual, publication; secondly there must be a section within the bibliography with a heading such as 'Religion', 'Church', 'Islam' or something similar; thirdly the section or sections must have at least a score or so of entries each year. We would like to hear from users of this *Guide* of any titles which fit these criteria and which they would like to see included in any future edition.

Michael J. Walsh

Heythrop College, London

Notes

1. *Library Association Record* 75, No. 2, 1973, pp. 21–22.

2. For these bodies, at least the main ones, *see* Otto Lankhorst's *Les Revues de Sciences Religieuses* (Strasbourg, Cerdic Publications, 1979), pp. 69–71.

3. *Bulletin of the Association of British Theological and Philosophical Libraries* (usually known simply as 'the ABTAPL *Bulletin*') New Series, No. 1, December 1974, p. 12.

4. It appears in March, June and November, and may be obtained from The Editor, ABTAPL *Bulletin*, New College Library, Mound Place, Edinburgh EH1 2LU, Scotland, U.K. Its ISSN is 0305-781X.

5. For the address of New College, *see* the previous note. For Birmingham: The Librarian, Central House, Selly Oak Colleges, 998 Bristol Road, Birmingham B29 6LE, U.K. For London: The Librarian, Heythrop College, 11–13 Cavendish Square, London W1M 0AN, U.K.

6. The Librarian, Dr. Williams's Library, 14 Gordon Square, London W.C.1, U.K.; The Librarian, Catholic Central Library, 47 Francis Street, London SW1P 1QR, U.K.

7. Volume 1 appeared in four parts, 1971–1972, and Volume 2 in two parts, 1973/4 and 1974/5.

8. An even more satisfactory compilation, for those with access to it, is the bi-monthly *Books in English*, now produced on microfiche and covering all books taken by the British Library in London and the Library of Congress in Washington.

9. One should perhaps also mention the section Catholic Church of the (American) *National Union Catalog, Pre-1956 Imprints* which was published as a separate item in 1970 by Mansell Information/ Publishing in London.

10. The *Index Bibliographicus* lists works by members of the Society of Jesus, most of which are not about the Society. For works on the Society, *see Archivum Historicum Societatis Iesu* (No. 29). The *Index* has not been included in this Guide.

11. The *Dictionnaire de Théologie Catholique* overcame this problem to some extent by publishing brief additional bibliographies in its index volumes.

How to use this Guide

There are 178 bibliographical tools of one sort or another to be found listed in this book. Some are well known, others less so. Some refer explicitly to one or other of the multitudinous different subject fields which may be contained under the general heading 'the study of religion'. A few of the entries are very general reference works which can be of particular use for religious studies. The entries are all listed in strict alphabetical order of title, and have been numbered. Users of this book are recommended to turn first to the Subject Index to find which of the entries will best help them in the kind of bibliographical search they wish to undertake.

On turning back from the Subject Index to the body of the book, the user will find the following information for each item listed:

(1) Title, followed by the standard abbreviation when one exists. Where appropriate, these abbreviations are taken from Siegfried Schwertner's *Internationales Abkürzungsverzeichnis für Theologie und Grenzgebiete*.[1]

(2) A subtitle, if this helps to explain the scope and purpose of the item under review.

(3) Bibliographical details – date of first publication, frequency and size. If the bibliography is cumulated, this is noted.

(4) Publishing history, where this is useful.

(5) Under the heading 'Arrangement' the layout of the publication is described. This is partly to help the user find his or her way round the publication, and partly to indicate the extent of the bibliographic content.

(6) 'Coverage' outlines the type of material covered by the bibliography under review – does it survey both books and periodical articles, are dissertations included, and so on. Either here, or under 'Arrangement' depending on the nature of the publication, will be discussed the subject or subjects within the general area of religious

studies which are included by the compilers in the bibliography under review.

(7) 'Comment' discusses the value of the indexing or abstracting service being examined. It will draw attention to the geographic spread of the material included, where this seems appropriate, to the standard of the periodicals scanned (are they learned journals or ephemera) and in particular remark upon the currency of the material included – how up-to-date it is.

(8) The publisher's name and address, and, if necessary, the editor or sponsoring body of the publication.

(9) The entry closes with the International Standard Serial Number (ISSN). The ISSN was not available for all the entries in this *Guide*.

The original intention was to include subscription prices at the end of each entry. However, in view of the constant changes that prices undergo because of such factors as inflation and currency fluctuations, it was felt that subscription information should be omitted.

Note

1. Berlin and New York: Walter de Gruyter, 1974. An expanded version has been published as a preliminary volume to *Theologische Realenzyklopädie* produced by the same publishers in 1976.

The Guide

1 Abortion Bibliography

Vol. 1– ; 1971–
Annual; no cumulations   23.5 cm

ARRANGEMENT: Each volume is in four major sections. The first section lists monographs, including government publications, on abortion; the second lists relevant periodical articles by title, and supplements this by a subject approach with over two hundred subject headings; the fourth section is an author index. These main sections are supplemented with a list of periodicals scanned (over 350 in the 1976 volume) and a subject-heading index. There is also a list of other secondary services which have been scanned to find relevant material. There are about 360 pages in a volume.

COVERAGE: The bibliography aims to cover all aspects of abortion. There is a special Religion and Ethics section which in 1976 had over 125 references. Most entries are for periodical articles, although one or two books and official publications are included. Most journals covered are in English, although German, French and some Slavonic material is present.

COMMENT: Most items in the 1976 volume (published 1978) are from journals published that year, though a few 1975 items are present. Where the original source was some other secondary service this is acknowledged. Although one of the best tools in the religion/medicine/ethics field, it is cumbersome to use because of the arrangement of periodical articles by their title. As all the information is repeated in the subject section (i.e., it is not a referral index, but simply repeats the information in the title sequence in a re-shuffled form), the title approach could well be abandoned. For any specialized library, it must be borne in mind that the *Abortion Bibliography* is intended to cover all abortion questions, and that the greater part of it is taken up with medical issues.

Published by the Whitston Publishing Co., P.O. Box 958, Troy, New York 12181, U.S.A.

2 Abstract Service [of the Institute on the Church in Urban–Industrial Society]

Vol. 1– ; 1970–

Monthly (with omissions); annual index (the index was quarterly till December 1977)   28 cm

ARRANGEMENT: Each issue of about 20 pages of duplicated typescript is entirely made up of abstracts (averaging 300 words), which are arranged in broad subject groupings. The subject headings are only given inside the front cover, with a numerical list of abstracts falling within each. Each abstract has an identification number. The annual index for 1978 contains a numerical sequence and title, author, and subject sequences. Copies of the documents abstracted can be obtained from I.C.U.I.S.

COVERAGE: Within the general field of Christian mission in urban and industrial areas, numerous specific topics are included, such as: industrial democracy, investment policy, housing, health care, education, employment, community organization and development, human rights, evangelism. The material included covers reports, reprints, conference papers, periodical articles, books. The latest issue has wide geographical coverage of North and South America, Africa and Asia, mainly of English language items. About 250 abstracts are published annually.

COMMENT: Most items are included within three months of publication, some within one month, and all within two years. Compilation is from an ecumenical, activist, point of view. The title of a conference reported from Varanasi, India, gives a significant description – 'Clergy as Prophets for Social Justice'.

Published for the Urban–Rural Mission Office, Commission on World Mission and Evangelism of the World Council of Churches, by the Institute on the Church in Urban–Industrial Society, 5700 South Woodlawn Avenue, Chicago, Illinois 60637, U.S.A.
ISSN 0362-059X

3 Abstracta Islamica (AbIsl)
Bibliographie selective des études islamiques
Vol. 1–   ; 1947–
Annual; no cumulations   23 cm

ARRANGEMENT: Published annually as a supplement to the
Revue des Études Islamiques since its inception in 1927, it now
forms a separate volume arranged in seven main subject
divisions, each one being sub-divided to fairly exact
headings. This is supplemented by an author index. A list of
periodicals covered is supplied inside the back cover. The
1974 volume (received 1978) has 141 pages.

COVERAGE: All aspects of Islam are surveyed, including
language, geography, and social sciences. Material of
religious interest can be found in all sections, but the most
useful heading is Islamologie. The section Bibliographie et
Documentation covers bibliographies, conference
proceedings, new periodicals and book reviews. There were
190 entries in the 1974 volume, and they date, for the most
part, from the previous year, though some earlier material
is present. The books and articles are mainly French,
though there are some German, Arabic and English.

COMMENT: There is a long delay between the cover date, the
date of the volume's arrival, and the date of publication of
the material covered. The numbering of the entries should
be noted: Section 3 is Islamologie; 3.5 is Soufisme, and all
entries under Soufisme are numbered 350001 and upwards.
The *Abstracta* is very useful for listing fairly obscure items,
and it is very scholarly in its organization. It is, however, a
poor second to the *Quarterly Index Islamicus* (No. 131), and
although entitled *Abstracta*, the entries vary from fairly long
abstracts to merely indicative entries.

Published for Fondation pour le Développement de l'Étude
de la Culture Arabe (FONDECA), by Paul Geuthner
Librairie Orientaliste, 12 Rue Vavin, 75006 Paris, France

4   Abstracts in Anthropology

Vol. 1– ;   1971/2–
Quarterly; no cumulations   23 cm

ARRANGEMENT: Each issue of *Abstracts in Anthropology* is arranged in four main sections: Archaeology (sub-divided regionally except for a general section); Cultural Anthropology (14 subject sub-divisions of which one is Symbol Systems – Religion, Ritual and World View); Linguistics (not sub-divided); Physical Anthropology (12 subject sub-divisions). Within each sub-section, the abstracts are arranged alphabetically by author. There are author and subject indexes in each issue and a list of the journal titles abstracted in the issue. Each entry carries an abstract of up to 200 words. Full author, title and journal details are given to each entry. Reference from the indexes is by running number.

COVERAGE: Subject coverage is indicated above, and material is gathered from some 200 English-language journals plus the occasional Festschrift and collected work. The scope is world wide. In the four issues for 1977/78, 3867 abstracts were included of which 136 were under the heading Symbol Systems. The subject index is quite detailed and lists many other abstracts on religious subjects not included in the Symbol Systems category. Thus: Religion (124), Ritual (94), Muslim (7). The only specifically religious journal abstracted is *History of Religions*.

COMMENT: Each issue relates to the year in question and inclusion seems prompt. The arrangement is clear and the index useful. No particular problems should be presented in using this publication. In general, *Abstracts in Anthropology* is very useful for the anthropological points of view of religion: the historical and social organization. Improvements are planned for Volume 8, including a 50 percent increase in coverage.

Published by the Baywood Publishing Company Inc., 120 Marine Street, Farmingdale, New York 11735, U.S.A.
ISSN 0001-3455

6

5 Abstracts of English Studies (AES)

Vol. 1– ; 1958–
Ten issues a year, the tenth being the annual index
23 cm

ARRANGEMENT: Brief editorial details, a synopsis of the classification adopted and a list of the journal issues abstracted are followed by the main classified section. There is a name and subject index to each issue and to the annual volume. The abstracts are arranged in four major sections: General; Britain; United States; World Literature in English and Related Languages. Each major section is further divided: the General section into General Studies, Bibliography, Languages, Themes and Types; and the other sections chronologically or by region. There are further sub-divisions down to individual authors (e.g. T. S. Eliot, J. H. Newman) or topics (e.g. Editing, Linguistics).

The abstracts are a paragraph in length and give the author and title of the article abstracted, and brief details of the source journal – fuller details are provided in the prefatory notes. Each abstract has a running key number and each is signed. There is no separate classification or category for religious subjects except that Bible, Religious Literature, Miracle and Morality Plays are index entries.

COVERAGE: Some 1500 journals and numerous monographs are screened for material dealing with American and English literature, world literature in English and related languages, and English language. The majority of the periodicals scanned are American. Religion is covered to the extent of how it influenced particular writers, how it helps to explain a writer's imagery and language, and, occasionally, a writer's religious viewpoint or contribution to religious issues. There were 3549 abstracts in Volume 21, or about 350 per issue.

The abstracts 'are designed to indicate the content of the article or monograph as concisely as possible and without editorial bias. The abstracts state the thesis, express the method of development, and point to major implications. Any subject mentioned in the abstract is covered significantly in the article.' (Preface).

COMMENT: The appearance of items in *AES* seems leisurely: three years is fairly common, while eight, and even ten years' delay is not unknown. *AES* is best used when material on a particular author or period is wanted, since otherwise approach must be through the index, which is rather limited for subject terms. A multi-annual cumulation is needed. Although perhaps borderline for many, *AES* would be useful for tracing religion in English literature from American sources, and thus complements the *Annual Bibliography of English Language and Literature* (No. 15).

Published by the National Council of Teachers of English, 1111 Kenyon Road, Urbana, Illinois 61801, U.S.A.
ISSN 0001-3560

6   Acta Ordinis Fratrum Minorum (AOFM)

Vol. 1–   ; 1882–
Six issues a year; no cumulations   30 cm

ARRANGEMENT: The journal consists mainly of the texts of the various decrees and documents relating to the Order. Languages used for this are, in the main, Latin, French or Italian. Each issue carries a section entitled Bibliographia in which are listed (a) books relevant to the study of the Order; (b) titles of periodicals with lists of their contents and (c) titles of periodicals with volume and part received. Entries in all sections are arranged alphabetically.

COVERAGE: The subject matter is mainly to do with the Order, or with areas in which it was, or is, operating. Books and periodicals in most Western languages appear, and there is also some material from Yugoslavia. The number of periodicals varies according to the number received by the Order in Rome. In the issue of March/April 1979, for example, 19 books were listed, together with the contents of 11 periodicals. Others were simply mentioned as 'received'. In addition there was a list of 52 journals and magazines published by the Order throughout the world.

COMMENT: *AOFM* is of limited use except for those studying the Order as such, and is very incomplete in the bibliographical information it supplies. It keeps fairly up to date in its coverage, but the selection of material is very specialized.

Published by Curia Generalis Ordinis, Via S. Maria Mediatrice 25, 00165 Roma, Italy
ISSN 0001-6411

7 **Actualidad Bibliográfica de Filosofía y Teología**
Selecciones de libros San Francisco de Borja
Vol. 1– ; 1964–
Semi-annual; no cumulations   23.5 cm

ARRANGEMENT: Each issue contains two or three scholarly articles. These are followed by reviews of recent books on various aspects of theology and philosophy. Finally, there is a section covering books with much shorter notes about them. The second issue of each year contains an author index to both issues for a year, and this includes all three sections already mentioned and authors referred to in the articles. The main book review section is arranged alphabetically by author, and the shorter notices are arranged in broad subject categories.

COVERAGE: Only books are covered, but the languages include Spanish, French, German and English. Subjects are mainly mainstream theology and philosophy of religion, although some other topics are included (for example, the sociology of medicine).

COMMENT: Nearly all the books in the main review section or the shorter notices are of recent date, and not only is the currency good but the issues arrive very promptly. The *Bibliográfica* is, therefore, a very helpful tool. All of the reviews, however, are in Spanish, and its main usefulness lies in its coverage of works in that language. Bibliographical information is excellently presented.

Published for Faculdades de Filosofía y Teología, San Francisco de Borja, by Ediciones Mensajero, S. Cugat del Valles, Barcelona, Spain
ISSN 0037-1181

8 ADRIS Newsletter

Vol. 1– ; 1971–
Quarterly; annual cumulations   27 cm

ARRANGEMENT: Following sections on the calendar of coming events, and news, announcements, organizations and directories, the bibliographical section is divided into four parts: (1) Bibliography, Information, Research, and Reference Matters; (2) From and About Serials and Periodicals; (3) Recent Noteworthy Articles; (4) Bulletin of Recent Books. Each section is arranged in essay form rather than as a list of books and articles, and there is no strict alphabetical arrangement. Publisher, date and ISBN number are given. At the end of every fourth volume an index of the titles (underlined), authors and editors (though not for articles in the periodical section), and periodical titles for the year is compiled.

COVERAGE: *ADRIS* is devoted to the goal of promoting coordination and cooperation among omni-media bibliography and information services and systems that deal with, or touch upon, religion. Thus its coverage is wide, with an emphasis on reference and research material in both Christian and non-Christian religions, and sometimes non-religious subjects. Most of the material is American, although English and French works are included. The bibliography section lists mainly reference works (yearbooks, directories etc.) and bibliographies. The periodicals' section lists new periodicals recently published, and then abstracts of chosen articles in various periodicals are given in the Recent Noteworthy Articles section. In the Bulletin of Recent Books, short appraisals of new books are given.

COMMENT: A valuable bibliography, especially for new works published in the U.S.A. and for new periodicals, it is especially useful for its listing of reference material. The rather loose format means that it is not as convenient to use as a more formal bibliography, although it must be remembered that it is described as a 'newsletter'; the typography and layout are also rather less than perfect. The

10

yearly index is rather sparse and does not include the abstracted periodical articles.

Published by the Department of Theology, Loyola University of Chicago, 6525 North Sheridan Road, Chicago, Illinois 60626, U.S.A.
ISSN 0300-7022

American Bibliography of Slavic and East European Studies

Vol. 1–   ; 1967–
Continues *American Bibliography of Russian and East European Studies*, 1956–1966
Annual   27 cm

ARRANGEMENT: The main section is a classified arrangement of journal articles and information on books. The subject areas within this section are fairly broad and one sub-section, XIV, is for Religion. A second section covers reviews of books and this is arranged in a parallel classification. There is a Biobibliographical Index which consists of names of the persons treated, and finally an Author Index.

COVERAGE: 'This bibliography seeks to present as complete a record as possible of North American publications in Slavic and East European studies ... but does not pretend to be comprehensive.' It covers books, book reviews, portions of books (e.g. parts of anthologies, Festschriften and collections), journal articles, review articles, dissertations. It is interdisciplinary in scope and over 700 journals are searched. In the 1973 volume there were 105 items on religion in the journal and books section, and 20 items in the book review section.

COMMENT: Given its limited subject scope, and the fact that only North American sources are used, the usefulness of this bibliography does seem a little restricted. The two- to three-year publishing delay also lessens its appeal. But provided other sources are used, such as the *Current Digest of the Soviet Press*, it could be useful for tracing material relating to this relatively poorly covered area (bibliographically speaking).

Published by the Library of Congress for the American Association for the Advancement of Slavic Studies, c/o The Editor, American Bibliography of Slavic and East European Studies, Slavic and Central European Division, Library of Congress, Washington D.C. 20540, U.S.A.

10   American Doctoral Dissertations

Vol. 1–   ; 1955/6–

Replaced *Doctoral Dissertations accepted by American Universities*, covering the period 1933/4 to 1954/5; from 1955/6 to 1963/4 it was called *Index to American Doctoral Dissertations*. Annual; no cumulations

ARRANGEMENT: The present version is arranged by an alphabetical sequence of broad subject headings and, under each heading, by university. The entries themselves are very brief, and indicate no more than author, full title and date. This subject arrangement is followed by an author index. Preliminary matter in each volume includes tables giving information about the publication and lending of dissertations, and the distribution of doctorates by university and subject field.

COVERAGE: The scope of the work is described by the Introduction: 'a complete listing of all doctoral dissertations accepted by American and Canadian universities. It is compiled from commencement programs issued by the universities ... It includes a number of dissertations which are not included in *Dissertation Abstracts International*, as well as a number which will be carried in later issues'. Over the last decade, 4217 dissertations in religion have been listed, out of the c. 35,000 which are included annually.

COMMENT: Currency is good, in that dates of degrees related closely to the years covered by the annual volumes, but over a year may elapse before the volume actually appears. The layout is poor, and the subject classification is too broad. Thus Theology is not sub-divided in any way apart from the arrangement by university, which in any case is for the most part irrelevant. The alphabetical arrangement of subject headings results in Religion being unhelpfully separated from Theology. As the fullest list of recent American doctoral dissertations, this work is unrivalled, but the poor subject indexing combined with the poor layout and brief entries make it difficult to use. The fuller abstracts and alternative title keyword indexing of *Dissertation Abstracts International* (No. 78) make the latter an essential complementary work of reference. For dissertations before 1973, the searcher is invited to use the *Comprehensive Dissertation Index 1861–1972* (No. 74). For British materials, the fullest listing is in the ASLIB *Index to Theses* (No. 94), but see also *Current Research*, (No. 77).

Published by University Microfilms International, P.O. Box 1764, Ann Arbor, Michigan 48106, U.S.A. *and* 18 Bedford Row, London, WC1R 4EJ, U.K.
ISSN 0065-809X

Analecta Bollandiana (AnBoll)
Revue critique d'hagiographie
Vol. 1– ; 1882–
Quarterly (in practice semi-annually, four issues published as two); no cumulations, four vicennial indexes   25 cm

ARRANGEMENT: Each issue contains between 225 and 250 pages, of which the major part (c. 60 percent) consists of some 12 scholarly articles, often separated by single-page fillers, devoted to hagiographical studies and research, and the publication of hitherto unpublished documents, the review supplementing the *Acta Sanctorum*. The remainder of each issue consists of a bibliographical section (c. 15 percent of the total); Bulletin des Publications Hagiographiques; a list of books received and, with the second issue, indexes and contents lists. From 1970 to 1976 there appeared numbered contributions to a series entitled Catalogues Récents de Manuscrits. Similar contributions have appeared since, but not apparently as part of this series. Neither the Bulletin nor the Catalogues occupy any special position in each issue.

COVERAGE: The Bulletins are not systematic. They consist of signed reviews and initialled short notices of books, part-works and series. The books noticed include not merely editions of, and research into, the lives of saints, but any major work with content likely to be of interest, and working tools such as palaeographical works. The Catalogues contain a series of short notices, usually by one person, of recent (within the last five years) catalogues of manuscript collections, each Catalogue being limited to manuscripts of a single language. The entries are arranged alphabetically by location. Saints figuring largely in the books noticed in the Bulletins or in the manuscripts of the Catalogues are indexed in the annual Index Sanctorum which, with its vicennial cumulations, is an important tool for those engaged in hagiographical studies.

COMMENT: The Bulletins are dependent upon works submitted for review, but such is the standing of the Bollandists that few serious works are missed. There are, however, sometimes delays of five years or more before books are noticed. Recourse to this journal, edited as it is by the compilers of the *Acta Sanctorum*, should be considered indispensable by all engaged in scholarly research into the lives of the saints.

Published by Société des Bollandistes, 24 Boulevard Saint-Michel, B-1040 Bruxelles, Belgium
ISSN 0003-2468

12   Anglo-Saxon England
Vol. 1–   ; 1972–
Annual; no cumulations   23 cm

ARRANGEMENT: The annual volume consists of a dozen or so scholarly articles followed by a bibliography for the year before the appearance of the volume.

COVERAGE: All aspects of Anglo-Saxon studies are included in the bibliography, but the student of religious history will find some of the headings of particular value, those on Anglo-Latin, for instance, or on the Liturgy and Latin ecclesiastical texts. The information is derived from the c. 70 periodicals which are regularly scanned, and from many other journals as well. The bibliography includes books, Festschriften and a separate section containing an index to relevant book reviews.

COMMENT: Currency is reasonable. As was indicated above, the bibliography is for the year prior to publication of *Anglo-Saxon England*, but the volume itself can come out quite late in the year, certainly in the second half. Occasionally earlier, obscure items find their way into the annual listing. The bibliography is very specialized, but by using the whole range of subject headings and not simply those with more obvious religious connotations, well over a hundred citations of interest to religious studies may be found each year.

Published by Cambridge University Press, P.O. Box 110, Cambridge CB2 3RL, U.K.

L'Année Philoligique (AnPh)
Bibliographie critique et analytique de l'antiquité gréco-latine
Vol. 1–   ; 1924/26–
Première année, covering 1924–1926, was published in 1928. Then annually from *2me* (1927) 1928–   , except for Volumes 15–17 (1940–1946), plus the following retrospective volumes: *Bibliographie classique 1896–1914*, ed. S. Lambrino, Part 1; auteurs et textes (only), 1951; *Dix années de bibl. classique 1914–1924*, ed. J. Marouzeau, 2 parts 1927–1928 (repr. 1969). Annual; no cumulations   24 cm

ARRANGEMENT: Each volume is a list of books and articles arranged in a systematic subject order. Volume 47 (*année* 1976) has 910 pages. The sequence of subjects is indicated in a Table des Divisions, and is preceded by an index of periodicals abstracted. The first division is one of classical authors (and titles of anonymous classical works); the second is divided into ten subject areas: I. Histoire Littéraire; II. Linguistique et Philologie; III. Histoire des

Textes; IV. Antiquités; V. Histoire; VI. Droit; VII. Philosophie; VIII. Sciences, Techniques et Métiers; IX. Les Études Classiques; X. Mélanges et Recueils. All of these are further sub-divided, and in each sub-division the arrangement is: (a) bibliographical and review articles; (b) editions; (c) collections, etc.; (d) studies. Within each of these groupings the entries are arranged in alphabetical order of the modern authors. There are indexes of: (1) collective titles (e.g. Hermetica, Liturgica); (2) ancient names; (3) geographical names; (4) humanists; (5) authors.

COVERAGE: Subjects are: ancient Greek and Latin literature, linguistics, history & antiquities, law, philosophy, religion, science and technology. Histoire Religieuse et Mythologie is arranged as a sub-division of Section V. Histoire. It is sub-divided into Generalia, Religions Diverses, Religions Comparées; Religion et Mythologie Grecque; Religion et Mythologie Romaine et Italique; Religion Judeo-Chrétienne. Under the last heading the reader is referred to the index of collective headings, e.g. Hymni Christiani; Liturgica Monastica. Books, dissertations and periodical articles (from approximately 950 periodicals) are indexed. Volume 47 (année 1976) has 11,573 entries of which 425 fall under the heading Histoire Religieuse. Entries are annotated in French, English or German.

COMMENT: The majority of entries in Volume 47, (année 1976, published in 1978) were published in 1976, others in 1974 and 1975. Individual reference numbers first appear in Volume 47; previously the references were from the index to page numbers. In spite of good printing, differentiation of headings by capitals, titles in italics, abstracts in roman, and section headings in bold capitals, the page is rather cluttered by a mass of print.

Christianity and other religions occupy a place in this bibliography ancillary to its main interests. Many of the entries in history, archaeology, patristics, liturgy, would be duplicated in other guides. But for the areas where the Graeco-Roman and Judaeo-Christian worlds overlap its thorough analysis and annotation is likely to be indispensable.

Published by Société d'Édition 'Les Belles Lettres', 95 Boulevard Raspail, Paris VIᵉ, France

Annual Bibliography of British and Irish History
Vol. 1– ; 1975–
Annual; no cumulations   22.5 cm

ARRANGEMENT: The entries in this *Bibliography* are arranged chronologically by historical topic, each period being divided by subject sub-headings, of which Religion is one, and there is a subject index at the end. The entries give only author and title of the books and journals, with a bibliographical reference.

COVERAGE: All aspects of British and Irish history are included, and the entries are taken, in the main, from journals, though there are also analyses of Festschriften and other similar publications. Some monographs by non-standard publishers are also included.

COMMENT: The volume for 1978 contained only material which was published in that year, though the volume itself came out late in 1979. Currency, therefore, is reasonable. The *Bibliography* scans only standard journals, so it is not very helpful for discovering the obscure and out-of-the-way material. On the other hand it brings together within one set of covers material from a number of well-known journals, and can thereby save the researcher time, but is not, perhaps, of enormous value to those engaged in religious studies.

Published for the Royal Historical Society, by Harvester Press, 16 Ship Street, Brighton, East Sussex, U.K.
ISSN 0308-4558

Annual Bibliography of English Language and Literature (ABELL)
Vol. 1– ; 1920–
Annual   22 cm

ARRANGEMENT: The 16,000 or so entries in this large

bibliography are arranged in alphabetical order of author within subject categories. The subject categories are themselves subsumed under broader groupings. The largest general grouping is that for English Literature, which is sub-divided by period (e.g. Old English; Sixteenth Century) and then by the types of literature (e.g. Anthologies; Homilies; Prose) and authors *as* subjects (e.g. J. H. Newman; Alcuin; William Tyndale). The current classification dates from the 1973 volume. Each individual entry gives author, title and brief bibliographical details of the book, article or thesis in question. A running number is also given which is used to refer to the entry from the indexes and from other related entries.

There are two indexes. The Index of Authors and Subjects '... consists for the most part of the names of authors, and titles of anonymous literary works, which appear as headings within the main section "English Literature" '. The Index of Scholars includes compilers, critics, editors, translators and reviewers. The six-page table of contents gives an outline of the classification used and shows the sub-sections of The English Language and the other smaller sections not listed in the Index of Authors and Subjects. Finally, there is a listing of the Sources Consulted with abbreviations.

COVERAGE: The coverage of *ABELL* is impressive. The sources consulted cover journals, newspapers, books, Festschriften and collections, bibliographies (including the *British National Bibliography* (No. 53)), theses (e.g. *ASLIB Index to Theses* (No. 93)) and dissertations (e.g. *Dissertation Abstracts International* (No. 78)): some 1277 sources altogether. A feature of *ABELL* is that references are made to reviews of many of the items indexed. Though the subject matter is *English* language and literature, the sources consulted are international, with a large number of foreign-language journals. (Translations of titles are provided). The quantity of items indexed is also impressive. The volume for 1974 listed 16,178 entries, which must make this the largest bibliography on its subject. How many of these entries relate to religious topics is hard to assess. Apart from the sections on The Bible, Religious Information and Instruction, and Saints' Lives, Legends, Exempla, which occur in the Middle English and Fifteenth Century section, it is a matter of looking up the entries under specific authors or specific works of a religious nature or interest. No indication is given of the criteria for inclusion in *ABELL*, although many important religious authors are included. Thus from the Sixteenth Century section we find William Tyndale, Sir Thomas More, Richard Hooker and Desiderius Erasmus; and from 'A' in Index of Authors and Subjects are found Aelfric, Ancrene Wisse, Anselm, Assumption of Our Lady, and Aurobindo. Apart from the problem of selection of authors, the items indexed relate to the author's works as bibliographic works seen within the context of linguistic and literary history. It is outside the scope of *ABELL* to consider, for instance, the place of these works in the context of religious or doctrinal history.

COMMENT: Many items indexed in the annual volume relate to previous years, the year of the title is published several years later (e.g. the volume for 1975 was published in 1978), and there is a further delay of six months or more for receipt. Thus work done on a subject in four years will not have been covered in *ABELL*. This is a distinct drawback. Further drawbacks are the fact that there is no cumulative indexing, and that the subject indexing is mostly concerned with personal names. However, if one is fortunate enough to be interested in someone that the compilers consider to be important enough to be indexed in *ABELL*, then the vast coverage of *ABELL* makes it an important resource. It could also prove useful to someone looking into the background of a certain period.

Published by the Modern Humanities Research Association, and obtainable from the Hon. Treasurer MHRA, King's College, Strand, London WC2R 2LS, U.K.
ISSN 0066-3786

16 Annual Bulletin of Historical Literature
Vol. 1– ; 1910–
Annual   21 cm

ARRANGEMENT: This is mainly by period, with three sections
devoted to history outside Europe. Most sections except the
non-European and twentieth-century ones have a
particular heading (Religion), or something similar. Each
section is arranged as a narrative rather than a list of
citations. There is an author index but no subject approach
other than that described.

COVERAGE: The *Bulletin* aims to bring together notices of the
main pieces of published research in the field of history,
regardless of subject or country. Both books and serials are
covered. Most Western languages are represented, although
the majority of the works cited are in English, and the
greater part of the *Bulletin* relates to Europe, with particular
emphasis on the United Kingdom.

COMMENT: The *Bulletin* is useful, but by no means
comprehensive. The narrative style obliquely provides a
sort of abstract-cum-evaluation of the items listed, and
makes for easy reading, but much material is omitted which
will have to be found through major national
bibliographies or *Historical Abstracts* (No. 189). Book citations
are usually adequate to trace the publisher, but some useful
publishing details are occasionally omitted. Citations for
periodicals are distinctly poor in quality. They omit the part
of the volume, and, invariably, the page reference. It is
impossible to estimate the number of items surveyed, but
the 1975 volume had 158 pages. In fairness to the *Bulletin* it
has to be said that its preface disclaims any attempt at
comprehensiveness, and its aim is to give a general picture
to librarians, university lecturers and teachers conducting
specialized courses of what is available. It is most useful in
identifying general trends in scholarship, and within those
trends religion is one.

Published by the Historical Association, 59A Kennington
Park Road, London S.E.11, U.K.
ISSN 0066-3832

Annuarium Historiae Conciliorum (AHC)
Internationale Zeitschrift für Konziliengeschichtsforschung
Vol. 1–   ; 1969–
Semi-annual; no cumulations   size varies

ARRANGEMENT: The *AHC* is a scholarly journal, publishing articles in various languages on all aspects of the history of councils of the Church. Most issues contain a bibliography, covering the same ground, with about 150 citations in each issue, organized by very broad subject headings.

COVERAGE: Journals in all languages are scanned to produce material, but the field of interest is very limited.

COMMENT: The *Annuarium* is a highly important journal within its chosen field, but the bibliographies which it publishes do not commend themselves. There is frequently a lengthy gap between the appearance of an article, and its citation in the *AHC*. It is a useful, but not essential tool, and does not compare well with the *Bulletin of Medieval Canon Law* (No. 59) as a bibliographical aid.

Published by Ferdinand Schöningh Verlag, Rathausplatz, Postfach 1020, D-479 Paderborn, Federal Republic of Germany
ISSN 0003-5157

Archaeological Bibliography for Great Britain and Ireland
Vol. 1–   ; 1950–
Annual   20 cm

ARRANGEMENT: There are two main sections. One is the Topographical Section which is arranged as an index in alphabetical order under each period and county. There is a reference number to the fuller information provided in the Author List. The Author List is an alphabetical listing of authors giving full bibliographic details.

COVERAGE: Material relating to Great Britain and Ireland from the earliest times to 1600 A.D. is covered. This material is derived from archaeological periodicals and county journals published in Great Britain and Ireland, general periodicals which contain articles or items of archaeological interest, books and monographs. Some 200 journals are covered and the actual issues are noted. Philology, genealogies and purely historical material are excluded.

COMMENT: As a moderately comprehensive listing of British archaeological material, this publication is important for anyone looking into the early religious history of Great Britain, or at the history of particular localities or buildings. Fuller information about many of the items listed will be found in *British Archaeological Abstracts* (No. 50). Publication delays are up to three years.

Published by the Council for British Archaeology, 112 Kennington Road, London SE11 6RE, U.K.
ISSN 0066-5967

19 Archief voor de Geschiedenis van de Katholieke Kerk en Nederland (AGKKN)

Vol. 1– ; 1959–
Semi-annual   21 cm

ARRANGEMENT: Each issue of the periodical contains four or five scholarly articles, and the second issue of a volume contains the bibliography. This is divided into several sections, the main principle of division being geography, although there are useful general and bibliographical sections at the beginning. Within each section arrangement is alphabetical by author. There is a combined index for the main articles and the bibliography.

COVERAGE: Both books and articles are included if they have any bearing on Church history in the Low Countries generally, and Holland in particular. Most items are in Dutch (Flemish), although English-language ones are also noted. For the 1977 bibliography, 32 periodicals were scanned, and some 250 entries were included, some of them dating from the two previous years.

COMMENT: It is difficult to draw many parallels, but this service seems as good as most of its kind for such a limited area, and provides the researcher with a relatively easy way of finding out what exists in the field. The coverage of periodicals is very good, and the *Archief* brings together books and serials in a handy format.

Published by Dekker & van de Vegt, Oranje Siergel 4, P.O. Box 256, Nijmegen, Netherlands
ISSN 0003-8326

Architectural Periodicals Index (API)
Vol. 1– ; 1972–

API is the published version of the British Architectural Library's own periodicals subject index, which is located at the Royal Institute of British Architects (RIBA). It supersedes the RIBA Library Review of Periodicals in *RIBA Journal*, 1933–1946, and the *RIBA Library Bulletin* (Q), 1946–1972. Annual cumulations date from 1965 as the *RIBA Annual Review of Periodical Articles*, which changed to the present title in 1972. There is no multi-annual cumulation, but a microfilm edition of the Library's card index to periodicals covering 1956–1970 is available from World Microfilms Publications.
Quarterly; annual cumulation   30 cm

ARRANGEMENT: *API* is arranged alphabetically by subject headings. Specific designs are entered under the appropriate building type and the heading extended to incorporate the country, particular locality and name of building or project if known. There are no cross-references, but entries are duplicated under different headings. The BAL List of Periodical Subject Headings provides a useful guide, and each issue of *API* (since January 1978) gives a List of Subject Headings used in the issue. In the 1977 volume, headings relevant to religion included Cathedrals (19 items); Chapels (15); Church Halls (2); Churches, and its sub-headings (30); Islamic Architecture (8); Synagogues (2).

The index entry itself consists of the title of the article (with English translations of foreign-language titles); the name of the architect etc. if given; the author of the article; the types of illustration; references to bibliographies and cost analyses; title of the periodical with volume and issue number, dates and pagination. Clarificatory notes are provided where necessary.

Each issue carries a Name Index of authors, architects, designers, organisations, etc., but not the name of buildings. The cumulative issue carries a Topographical Index (since January 1978). Each issue gives not only a list of the periodical titles indexed, but exactly which issues. Each entry carries a running number for cross-reference purposes.

COVERAGE: *API* is based on the holdings of the British Architectural Library, which is one of the world's greatest collections of architectural information. The aim of *API* is to be an up-to-date general, though selective, index to some 300 of the world's architectural periodicals. The subjects covered include architecture and allied arts, design and environmental studies, landscape, planning, and relevant research. Articles on current practice and historical themes are included. 'Every attempt is made to cover architecture world wide and periodicals from some 45 countries are at present indexed. However, a greater emphasis is placed on architecture and design in Great Britain and all projects and designs in Great Britain, executed or unexecuted, as well as British work abroad are indexed when significant information, i.e. more than mere notes, is supplied.' Book reviews, letters and news items are generally omitted.

COMMENT: *API* is produced promptly and most entries are recent. Since January 1978, the index is computer produced and microforms, magnetic tapes and a Card Reproduction Service were expected to be introduced in 1979. Photocopies of articles indexed are obtainable from the British Architectural Library. For those concerned with the planning and design of religious buildings, *API* would seem to be an essential resource. It should also be of interest to those studying the history of religious buildings in general, or certain buildings in particular, since historical accounts are included.

Published for the British Architectural Library, by RIBA Publications Ltd., Finsbury Mission, Moreland Street, London EC1V 8VB, U.K.
ISSN 0033-6912

1 Archiv für Katholisches Kirchenrecht (AKathKR)

mit besonderer Rücksicht auf die Länder deutscher Zunge
Vol. 1–   ; 1857–
Semi-annual; no cumulations   25 cm

ARRANGEMENT: Each issue is divided into eight sections: major articles, short articles, ecclesiastical enactments and decisions, civil enactments and decisions, Church and State, Canon Law chronicle, reviews and notices, bibliography and list of books received. In addition the second issue of each year contains an index to contributors and a detailed index of contents. There are over 350 pages in each issue, of which the first two sections (articles) account for forty percent of the total, the next four (current civil and ecclesiastical law) take up another forty percent, and the last two sections (reviews and bibliography) about fifteen percent. Sections 3, 4 and 5 are each divided into two. In the first, extracts (fully cited) from major documents are provided; in the second, under appropriate subject headings, are descriptions of other major documents and where to find them. Not surprisingly, documents cited tend to be either Roman or locally generated. Section 6 details important pronouncements, or events arranged by date in subject groups. The contents of Section 8, the bibliographical section, are also distributed in established subject groups, not all of which recur in successive issues. Groups include Generalia, History of Canon Law, Current Law, Eastern Churches, Vatican II, Church and State, Evangelical Church Law. Wherever necessary groups are further divided.

COVERAGE: As one might expect, *AKathKR* is concerned primarily with changes and developments in ecclesiastical and civil law as they affect the Roman Catholic clergy in Germany. Legislation from the Vatican which affects the

Church internationally is obviously included, but legislation which does not affect the German clergy is not normally given unless some special significance can be demonstrated. The strong national orientation of this journal is reflected in the lack either of a list of *sigla* or of periodicals and series indexed. The editors clearly expect their readers to be acquainted with the literature. It is not possible to assess with any ease the extent of the *AKathKR*'s data base, but it appears extensive if largely European and German-language biased. No obvious gaps were noted.

COMMENTS: Current material is quite strongly featured, but is given significant support by material published over the last five years. *AKathKR* is impressive, the scholarship of the original contributions being matched by the thorough and systematic compilation and exploitation of the literature of the subject. It is probably not of enormous interest or use to the non-German reader. One minor irritation is that the abbreviations of the citations do not always conform to *IATG*.

Published by Verlag Kirchheim & Co., Mainz/Rhein, Federal Republic of Germany
ISSN 0003-9160

22 Archiv für Kirchengeschichte von Böhmen-Mähren-Schlesien (AKGB)

Vol. 1– ; 1967–
Irregular, but approximately every 1–2 years   24 cm

ARRANGEMENT: Each volume has over a dozen scholarly articles, and expositions of historical texts. These are followed by a book review section, and finally by the bibliography. The bibliography itself is arranged in four or five very broad subject divisions, and within these alphabetically by author. There are no indexes.

COVERAGE: The scope extends to any aspect of Church history in Bohemia or Silesia. Most of the items cited are in German or Czech, and only seven periodicals (including

AKGB itself) are covered, though a number of series are also entered when relevant.

COMMENT: The 1977 volume contained a number of items published as far back as 1972, though in such a specialized subject-field it is better that they are listed late than listed nowhere at all. The lack of indexes, either of author or subject, is hardly a disadvantage as the number of entries per year (c. 100) is very small.

Published by Institut für Kirchengeschichte Böhmen-Mähren-Schlesien, Bischoff Kaller Strasse 36, D-6240 Königstein, Federal Republic of Germany
ISSN 0570-6726

3 Archiv für Liturgiewissenschaft (ALW)
Vol. 1– ; 1950–
Continues *Jahrbuch für Liturgiewissenschaft*, Münster, Volumes 1–15; 1921–1941.
Annual (in publisher's binding); no cumulations, but index to Volumes 1–19, (1950–1977)   24 cm

ARRANGEMENT: Volumes have varied appreciably in length but over the last ten years have averaged slightly more than 500 pages. The contents are usually distributed in four sections: major articles, miscellanea, literature bulletin and indexes. The size of each section varies from volume to volume, but the third part has always the largest share, with fifty to seventy percent of the contents. It is the third section which probably is of most interest, but it should be noted that the second section has been used to carry N. K. Rasmussen: *Some Bibliographies of Liturgists* (1969), *Bibliographies of Liturgists: a First Supplement* (1973) and ... *a Second Supplement* (1977). The contents of the third section are organized under standard headings, although not every sub-section is represented in each volume. Headings, in German of course, include Liturgy in the Old and in the New Testament; Liturgy from the Carolingian period to Trent; Monastic Liturgy; Pastoral Liturgy; Liturgical Dialogue with Protestant Churches; Liturgy and Architecture; Liturgy after Vatican II, and so on. Each sub-section is further broken down by headings. That on the liturgy from Trent to Vatican II, for example, is divided as follows: General Works, Introductions, Collected Works; Liturgical Setting and Furnishing, Fittings and Vestments; Liturgical Year; Liturgy of the Word; Liturgy of the Sacraments; Liturgy of Sacramentals.

COVERAGE: All aspects of the liturgy are considered from a Roman Catholic viewpoint. *ALW* is edited from the Benedictine monastery of Maria Laach, and many contributors are members of that religious order, but the liturgical content is by no means exclusively Roman Catholic – other Christian and non-Christian liturgies come within its scope. Every item surveyed is numbered. Volume 19 contains, somewhat exceptionally, 1966 items in Section 3 which occupies 564 out of 790 pages. The list of *sigla* – which conforms to *IATG* – of periodicals and series cited, while not comprehensive is indicative of the coverage. It contains nearly 200 items, of which two-thirds are German-language, and the remainder are almost all European.

COMMENT: The literature surveyed is by no means up to date. In each sub-section there is a spread of five to six years, giving a distinctly retrospective flavour. In the treatment of its subject, however, *ALW* is in a class of its own, but access to the contents is likely to prove difficult without some knowledge of the German used throughout.

Published by Verlag Friedrich Pustet, Regensburg, Federal Republic of Germany
ISSN 0066-6386

24 Archiv für Reformationsgeschichte. Beiheft: Literaturbericht / Archive for Reformation History. Supplement: Literature Review (ARG.E)
Vol. 1– ; 1972–
The main journal has been publishing research articles twice a year since 1904. It carried a regular section in each issue from Volumes 42–62 (1951–1971) entitled

Zeitschriftenschau (arranged by subject and geographical region). This was not cumulated or indexed.

Annual; no cumulations, but Register/Index for Volumes 1–5 (1972–1976)   23 cm

Arrangement: Each *Supplement* volume is an annual index with annotations or abstracts to new publications. Volume 7 (1978) has 206 pages. Entries are arranged with running numbers in systematic subject order, under headings in German. There is a list of the headings used showing the arrangement of subjects, followed by geographical regions. The Index volume contains, in three sequences, five-year indexes of authors, names (of people discussed) and places.

COVERAGE: 'An international journal concerned with the history of the Reformation and its significance in world affairs' (Editorial statement). The coverage includes: Ecclesiastical History of Sixteenth-Century Europe; Protestant Reformation; Catholic Reform and Counter-Reformation; Luther, Zwingli, Calvin; Anabaptists; Cultural Aspects of the period, such as philosophy, political theory, art, music, literature, humanism. These are followed by a parallel series of country and regional sub-divisions. Coverage extends to periodical articles, books, dissertations, in German, French, English, Italian, Dutch, Danish, Hungarian, from all European and English-speaking countries. Signed abstracts or annotations are in German or English.

COMMENT: Most entries in Volume 7 (1978) are from 1977, others being dated 1975 or 1976. Knowledge of German is desirable in using this serial, but not as essential as it might be for a detailed study of the periods and regions covered. It is a more effective tool for its specific purpose than the *Bibliographie* of the *Revue d'Histoire Ecclésiastique* (No. 152).

Published under the auspices of the Verein für Reformationsgeschichte and the American Society for Reformation Research, by Gütersloher Verlagshaus Gerd Mohn, Königstrasse 23, Postfach 2368, Gütersloh, Federal Republic of Germany and American Society for

Reformation Research, 6477 San Bonita, St. Louis, Missouri
63105, U.S.A.
ISSN 0341-8375

25 Archives de Sciences Sociales des Religions (AS Rel)

Vol. 1– ; 1956–
Volumes 1–34 entitled *Archives de Sociologie des Religions*
Quarterly; each volume covering six months   24 cm

ARRANGEMENT: Principal material is scholarly articles on
sociology of religion in French with abstracts in English.
Each volume has about 320 pages. Second issue of each
volume (i.e. twice a year) has a Bulletin Bibliographique.
The Bulletin Bibliographique is divided into: (1) Bulletin des
Périodiques, an index to periodical articles, some with brief
annotations, arranged in alphabetical order by the name of
the author of the article; (2) Bulletin des Ouvrages, a series of
short book reviews also arranged by author's name and
signed in full by the reviewer. The periodical index entries
and the book reviews are numbered in one consecutive
sequence. There is no subject arrangement, but this is
provided in the cumulative indexes Tables Signalétiques for
Volumes 31–42 (1971–1976).

COVERAGE: Christianity, Judaism and all other religions and
religious movements seen from the social scientist's point of
view. Economics, politics, law, psychology, sociology,
anthropology, applied to religion. There are about 500
entries (taking book reviews and periodical articles together)
in each half year. The reviews are in French, the items
reviewed mainly in French, English, or German and
published in Europe or North America.

COMMENT: Periodical entries from the previous six months
are listed. Books reviewed date mostly from the previous
12–24 months, with a few from earlier years included. The
policy of publishing the subject indexes only in the
quinquennial index limits the use of this otherwise excellent
guide to an unsystematic browsing facility, however
comprehensive.

Published by Éditions du Centre National de la Recherche Scientifique, 15 Quai Anatole France, 75700 Paris, France

26 Archivo Teológico Granadino (ATG)

Organo del Centro de Estudios Postridentinos de la Facultad de Teología de la Compañia de Jesús de Granada
Vol. 23– ; 1960–
Annual   24 cm

ARRANGEMENT: Each volume has about 500 pages, of which the bulk is given to scholarly articles. About 150 pages form the Bibliografia which is subdivided into: (1) Boletin de Historia de la Teología en el periodo 1500–1800 – with three sub-sections for: studies of individuals (e.g. Melanchthon, Molinos, St. Thomas More); the Council of Trent; History of Theology (each with sub-headings e.g. Geography, Jansenism, Jesuits); then (2) Otras Obras – with eleven sub-sections for Sagrada Escritura, Patrología, Teología Dogmatica, Historia de la Teología, Historia de la Iglesia, Derecho Canonico, Espiritualidad, Liturgia, Filosofia, Historia, Varia; and finally (3) Index of authors and titles of works reviewed. There is a list of the contents of the volume which gives the above outline of subjects.

COVERAGE: The Bibliografia covers books and periodical articles. The reviews, which are signed, are all in Spanish. The items reviewed are in Spanish, Italian, German, French and English and originate mainly in European countries.

COMMENT: Most of the books reviewed in the 1978 volume were published in 1976 or 1977, with a few from 1975 or 1978. A scholarly book reviewing service in this specialized field. Selection and reviewing are naturally from a Roman Catholic viewpoint. Systematically organized for the finding of books on specific subjects, but without cumulated indexing.

Published by Consejo Superior de Investigaciones Científicas, Instituto Francisco Suárez, Medinaceli 4, Madrid, Spain *and* Facultad de Teología, Apartado 2002, Granada, Spain

27 Archivum Bibliographicum Carmelitanum (ABC)
Vol. 1– ; 1951–
Irregular   23.5 cm

ARRANGEMENT: Most volumes contain a Bibliographia Carmeli Teresiani for the previous years, and some include other bibliographical material – lists of texts and other documents – but this feature is absent from the recent volume. The main bibliography was, at one time, arranged by subject, with sub-divisions as necessary, but this has been dropped in favour of one single alphabetical sequence in which authors, persons or places, together with anonymous books or articles, are listed together. So articles about people or places usually appear twice, once under the subject and again under the author. There is, therefore, no index of author or subject.

COVERAGE: Broadly, anything to do with the Carmelite Order. Books, serials, reviews and primary documents are all included. There is no list of periodicals scanned, but the number is clearly impressive, and most Western European languages are included.

COMMENTS: This is a huge bibliography. Volumes 19–22, published in 1979, contain the bibliography for 1973–1976, and have over 4500 main entries. Despite the dates set, items from as far back as 1967 have been found in the combined volumes. Items which had been missed were usually listed in a supplement, but this has now been abandoned in favour of a single sequence. Numbering is continuous from the beginning of the bibliography, so the latest entry is No. 24,431. The new layout is off-putting, and would seem, from the point of view of information retrieval, to be less efficient. No detailed approach by subject is now possible, though the fact that the subject headings used to be in Latin (the few remaining ones still are) may have meant that its usefulness was limited to those with a grasp of that language. So *ABC* leaves a good deal to be desired in presentation and layout, but it is well printed, and undoubtedly comprehensive.

Published by Edizioni dei Padri Carmelitani Scalzi, Corso d'Italia 38, 00198 Roma, Italy
ISSN 0570-7242

8 Archivum Franciscanum Historicum (AFH)

Vol. 1– ; 1908–
Four issues a year in two parts, i.e. Fasc. 1–2 January–June, Fasc. 3–4 July–December   24 cm

ARRANGEMENT: This journal includes a substantial bibliographical section (Notae Bibliographicae) which is more in the nature of a book review section. There is no classified arrangement or subject index, only an author index.

COVERAGE: As a large listing of books and journal articles on all aspects of Franciscana, this source seems worthy of inclusion in this guide to indexing and abstracting tools. Each of the 150 to 200 items a year is given a page-length review. The sources come from many countries, although most reviews are in French.

COMMENTS: This is a useful current awareness tool on all aspects of the subject field and usefully supplements *Bibliographia Franciscana* (No. 34) which is still concentrating on 1964–1973 material. For browsing more than systematic searching.

Published by Collegio S. Bonaventura, Colle S. Antonio, 00046 Grottaferrata (Roma), Italy
ISSN 0004-665

9 Archivum Historicum Societatis Iesu (AHSJ)

Vol. 1– ; 1932–
Semi-annual; no cumulations; but index to Volumes 1–20; 1932–1951; Volumes 21–30; 1952–1961   24 cm

ARRANGEMENT: Over the last ten years each volume has contained an average of about 500 pages, with its contents indexed, but not grouped, under six headings: historical articles; unpublished texts; short articles; books reviewed; bibliography of the history of the Society and news items relating to Jesuit historiography. In addition to the index organized under these headings there is an alphabetical index, by author, of books reviewed. As well as the bibliographical section normally to be found after the book reviews in the second issue of each year, bibliographical articles on special topics occasionally figure among the short articles. The second issue of 1978 contained, for example, G. R. Dimler's 'A Bibliographical Survey of Jesuit Emblem Authors in French Provinces, 1618–1726'. The bibliographical section accounts for 15–20 percent of the contents, and begins with an index which distributes the contents of this section into seven sub-sections: auxiliary sciences; general history; Ignatius Loyola; cultural history (further divided); history by country, with a list of establishments appended; biographies, with a list of biographies appended; listings, by author, of books previously reviewed in *AHSJ* (references given) and now reviewed elsewhere (references given). This is followed by an author index to the bibliographical section with references (each item in this section is numbered). The number of items in the bibliographical section naturally varies from volume to volume, but averages about 1000.

COVERAGE: All aspects of Jesuit history appear to be covered, but there is no hint given of the extent of the data-base from which the bibliographical section is compiled (unlike, for example, the *Revue d'Histoire Ecclésiastique* (No. 152)). Monographs, part-works, series, periodicals, dissertations certainly figure, and in a wide variety of languages, a reflection, no doubt, of the world-wide commitment of the Jesuit apostolate and the geographical spread of the compilers.

COMMENT: In the volume for 1978 there were listed an impressive number of 1977 publications, a smaller number of 1975 and 1976 citations, and refreshingly few earlier references. This journal has no serious competitors, and it is pleasant to report that without the incentive of competition the structure of the bibliographical section and the facilities offered give evidence of careful attention to the needs of the user. While the journal has a Latin title, it might be pointed out that the contributions are multi-lingual.

Published by AHSJ, Via dei Penitenzieri 20, 00193 Roma, Italy

0 Archivum Historiae Pontificiae (AHP)
Vol. 1– ; 1963–
Annual; no cumulations   25 cm

ARRANGEMENT: The *AHP* publishes about half-a-dozen articles a year, and about twice that number of book reviews, on papal history and related topics. The bibliographical section follows these. Each annual volume contains some 700 or so pages, of which slightly under half are devoted to the bibliography and its indexes.

The bibliography is arranged in six sections. The first, Generalia, is further broken down into sub-sections on archives (those of the Vatican being treated separately), general works on the papacy, studies of papal power, of individual bishops and dioceses, of the liturgy, of councils, Canon Law, the status of the papacy and papal diplomacy and so on. One sub-section covers the city of Rome itself. The remaining five main sections are arranged chronologically with sub-sections under each pope, although again each section begins with general works covering the period. The second of the main divisions includes everything which illustrates the history of Christianity in Rome. The sub-sections are not standardized, but correspond to the particular needs of the period being covered. The final sub-section of each main division of the bibliography lists book reviews.

COVERAGE: The main subjects covered are, therefore, the popes (by name), the history of the papacy as an institution, Rome, Christian archaeology, art and liturgy, the councils of the Church and the general theological problems relating to the papacy, in particular papal primacy, infallibility, the papal *magisterium* and collegiality. The bibliography includes

35

not only periodicals – there is a list of those scanned – and monographs, but also encyclopaedias, Festschriften and other collections of articles, and dissertations as they appear in *Dissertation Abstracts International* (No. 78). Approximately 400 periodicals are surveyed, mainly Western European and American (both North and South), but some from Eastern European countries are listed, especially those from Poland, Rumania and, of course, Russia. The annual volume runs to some 3300 entries, not including those drawing attention to book reviews or 'recensiones'. The listing of 'recensiones' is limited to reviews of works which have themselves been included in earlier volumes of the *AHP*. Given the subject-matter of the bibliography there is, not unnaturally, a Roman Catholic bias in the selection of periodicals and books, but publications by those of other denominations (and none) are also covered, though not so exhaustively.

COMMENT: The volume for 1976/7 was published at the end of 1977, and was not generally available until about March 1978. Although most entries do indeed date from the period explicitly covered, the bibliography picks up a good many items it has missed from earlier years. There are very good author and subject indexes, and the method of numbering the entries enables the user to select fairly quickly from a group of entries in the index those items which most directly concern the period he is researching. Instructions for use are given in English and French as well as Latin, and although the headings for the various sections of the bibliography, and many of the entries in the index, are given only in Latin, this should cause little difficulty even for those who know little or nothing of that language.

For the history and theology of the papacy, or of individual popes, at particular periods this is an excellent compilation. Good though it is, however, both the historical and the theological material it covers are dealt with satisfactorily elsewhere (e.g., in the *Revue d'Histoire Ecclésiastique* (No. 152)). If the *AHP* were to be considered for purchase *solely* on the basis of its bibliography, then it might be thought something of a luxury in any library hard-pressed for funds.

Published by Facultas Historiae Ecclesiasticae, Pontificia Universitas Gregoriana, Piazza della Pilotta 4, 00187 Roma, Italy
ISSN 0066-6785

1 **Ateismo e Dialogo**
Vol. 1– ; 1966–
Quarterly   27.5 cm

ARRANGEMENT: *Ateismo e Dialogo* contains a number of fairly brief, generally non-scholarly, articles on the problems of the unbeliever. These are followed by the bibliography, organized under broad subject headings.

COVERAGE: All aspects of unbelief are taken into account, and both books and journals in most European languages are scanned to produce about three hundred entries in each issue.

COMMENT: This is an unusual, rather out-of-the-way sort of topic, and it is quite well covered by this periodical.

Published by Secretariato per il Non-Credente, 00120 Città del Vaticano, Italy

2 **Bibliografia Missionaria (BgMiss)**
Vol. 1– ; 1935–
The first volume was published in *Guida della Missione Cattoliche* for 1935, covering the year 1933. The *BgMiss* was first published as an independent volume in 1937, covering the year 1936. Between 1926 and 1934 an earlier version of the *BgMiss* appeared under the heading Missions-bibliographischer Bericht and variant titles in *Zeitschrift für Missionswissenschaft*.
Annual   23.5 cm

ARRANGEMENT: After a few general headings, the bibliography is divided for the most part into broad geographical areas, some being specific countries, others whole continents. There are two indexes, one of authors

37

and persons mentioned, the other of subjects and places. Most items cited are from journals, though some series are covered. Some entries contain brief informative abstracts, but for the most part only basic bibliographical information is included. The bibliography is followed by a book review section covering literature published in most Western languages, and from all parts of the world. Each of the reviews has full bibliographical details, and generally also a long abstract of the work. Most issues of the *BgMiss* have a supplementary section giving a list of documents concerned with the missions, and also the Atti Ufficiali of the Congregation for Evangelization and Propagation of the Faith.

COVERAGE: All aspects of missiology are covered in depth, and most languages are included. The coverage of journals is extensive, and embraces journals of all levels from scholarly periodicals to fairly lightweight but nonetheless informative missionary bulletins. The 1977 volume had 2027 entries for periodicals and short notes of books, together with 69 abstracts of more important books. The monographs included had come from countries such as Ceylon, Papua-New Guinea, and a number of African nations, as well as from Europe and North America. Nearly all the entries had been published in 1977, and the volume containing them appeared in mid-1978, although a small number of articles which had been missed in the previous volume were also mentioned.

COMMENT: Although there may be a problem with language – the introduction and summaries are all in Italian – the *BgMiss* is one of the very best tools in the field of missiology. The indexing is good, and the layout in general very clear. It covers some very obscure periodicals which may not be readily available in this country, but at least it alerts the user to the possibilities for further study and research. The *BgMiss* should ideally be used in conjunction with the *Bulletin of the Scottish Institute for Missionary Studies* (No. 60), which provides better coverage of books, but is often slower than the *BgMiss* to appear.

Published by Pontificia Biblioteca Missionaria della S. Congregazione per l'Evangelizzatione dei popoli, Pontificia Università Urbiana, Via Urbano VIII 16, 00165 Roma, Italy

Bibliografía Teológica Comentada

Vol. 1–   ; 1973–
Annual; no cumulations   21.5 cm

ARRANGEMENT: The well over five thousand citations of books and articles which appear in this bibliography are divided into a dozen major classes, with numerous subdivisions. Most of the entries give little more than the basic bibliographical information, but a number have very short abstracts as well. There are indexes to subjects, authors and biblical references.

COVERAGE: All aspects of 'Iberoamerican' theology and its relevance to the world today are covered by the *Bibliografía*, and most of the 400 journals scanned are in Spanish or Portuguese, although some French and Italian publications are included.

COMMENT: This is the major bibliography for the Latin-American theological student, and for anyone who wishes to keep up to date with developments in theological thinking in that fast-changing area of the world. Currency is reasonable. Items appear in the *Bibliografía* the year after their first publication as a general rule, although some older material is included. However, the *Bibliografía* does not usually appear until the very end of the year, so the time lag can be anything from 10 to 22 months.

Published by Instituto Superior Evangélico de Estudios Teológicos, Camacuá 282, 1406 Buenos Aires, Argentina

Bibliographia Franciscana (BgF)

Vol. 1–   ; 1942–
Bibliographia Franciscana is an annual bibliographic supplement to *Collectanea Franciscana*.
Annual   24 cm

ARRANGEMENT: The bibliography is unfolding as the annual instalments are issued. To date, the main categories are: I. Subsidia et Instrumenta; II. Relationes de S. Francisco; III. Relationes de Studiis et Doctrinis; IV. Relationes de Historia Primi Ordinis Franciscani. There are many divisions and sub-divisions, for example:

IV. Relationes de Historia Primi Ordinis Franciscani.
    A. De Historia Franciscana Universali.
       4. De Ordine Fratrum Minorum Conventualium.

Each entry gives title and author, brief bibliographic details, a running number, and occasionally, contents or explanatory notes. To date, the four annual issues cover 6277 entries.

COVERAGE: This bibliography covers Franciscan history and the life and work of St. Francis of Assisi. It aims to cover all published material – books, journal and Festschrift articles – published in the years in question. Latin, French, German, Italian and English languages are covered. The current volume, XIII, covers works published from 1964–1973; and to date, covers four of the annual supplements. Previous collections of annual volumes cover earlier years.

COMMENT: The fullest listing of Franciscan material, but needs to be supplemented by more recent publications such as those reviewed in *Archivum Franciscanum Historicum* (No. 29). The complex and detailed classification requires some mastering.

Published by the Istituto Storico dei Frati Minori Cappuccini, G.R.A. km 68.800, 00163 Roma, Italy

35 Bibliographia Internationalis Spiritualitatis (BIS)
Vol. 1– ; 1966–
Annual; no cumulations   23.5 cm

ARRANGEMENT: This bibliography of international spirituality covers some 500 pages and is arranged in eight main subject sections as follows: General, Biblical, Doctrinal, Liturgical, the Spiritual Life, Historical, Arts and

Spirituality, and Connected Disciplines. Each section is further sub-divided and all of the sub-divisions are tabulated at the beginning of the volume. Within each sub-division items are entered under author in alphabetical order. Each entry is given a running number and this is used as a basis for all references. Full bibliographical details are provided in each entry. An index of authors is provided at the end of the volume.

COVERAGE: The *BIS* is a Catholic publication and as such the emphasis is on Christianity and particularly Catholic spirituality and theology. It is comprehensive in its coverage. One section is devoted to non-Christian religions. This covers some 15 pages and contains around 250 entries. A list of some 475 journals indexed is provided and this includes all the major American and European titles. The text of the bibliography is in Latin and the entries themselves span various languages. In the volume examined there were some 6823 entries covering periodical articles and books.

COMMENT: The volume examined was that for 1975. This was published in 1978 and received by the holding library in 1979. Therefore, although the entries do relate to 1975 publications, the bibliography is in effect up to four years out of date by the time it reaches the library shelves. The classified arrangement with the separate author index is perhaps not as convenient in such a large publication as one general subject/author listing. However, the publication is not as formidable as it may seem at first sight and the running numbers which are used as the basis for all reference stand out quite clearly. Despite the length of time it takes for each volume to appear, the *BIS* is a valuable reference tool for major libraries.

Published by the Pontificio Istituto di Spiritualità, Edizioni dei Padri Carmelitani Scalzi, Corso d'Italia 38, 198 Roma, Italy
ISSN 0084-7836

36 Bibliographia Patristica (BPatr)

Internationale patristiche Bibliographie
Vol. 1– ; 1959–
Annual; no cumulations   24 cm

ARRANGEMENT: The whole volume forms the bibliography. Entries are arranged in classified subject order. The headings are in Latin with sub-division alphabetically by author. Preliminaries are in German. There is a list of periodicals with abbreviations (approximately 1250 titles). Entries are numbered consecutively. There is also a separately numbered sequence of index entries to book reviews. The volume ends with an index of authors (or articles etc.) with references by number to the main entries.

COVERAGE: The scope of the bibliography is as follows: Writings of the Fathers of the Church (Eastern till A.D. 787; Western till A.D. 667); New Testament; New Testament Apocrypha; Christian Doctrine; Philosophy; Liturgy; Creeds; Exegesis of Old and New Testament; Gnosticism; Hagiography. It covers books, dissertations and periodical articles, and is without annotations. There are 2485 entries, plus 934 book review entries in Volume 16/17 and many cross-references (i.e. one item is often indexed under more than one heading). The entries are mainly in European languages and from many countries (but also include Japanese).

COMMENT: Published as a bound volume. Publications of 1971 and 1972 are indexed in Volume 16/17, which was not published till 1978; Volume 1 itself was not published until 1959. The obvious disadvantage of this bibliography is the extent to which it is in arrears. For its subject field it is nevertheless the most thorough and easy to consult. The *Bibliographie* of the *Revue d'Historie Ecclésiastique* (No. 152) is its nearest rival. This has fewer entries on this range of subjects, and retrieval is more difficult from its more general classification. But if plans being made at the Faculté de Théologie, Université Laval, Québec, Canada, come to fruition, there will soon be a notable competitor in their Banque d'Information Bibliographique en Patristique

(BIBP). This is a computer-based data bank which is recording the analysis of over 2000 periodicals, plus monographs, theses, etc. It is planned that the information will be kept up to date, and be available for consultation in a variety of ways, based on the use of key-words, authors, titles, and combinations of all these.

Published for the Patristische Komission der Akademien der Wissenschaften in der Bundesrepublik Deutschland, by Walter de Gruyter & Co., Genthiner Strasse 13, D-1000 Berlin 30, Federal Republic of Germany, *and* 200 Saw Mill River Road, Hawthorne, New York 10532, U.S.A.

Bibliographic Index
A cumulative bibliography of bibliographies
Vol. 1: 1937–1942; Vol. 2: 1943–1946; Vol. 3: 1947–1950; Vol. 4: 1951–1955; Vol. 5: 1956–1959; Vol. 6: 1960–1962; Vol. 7: 1963–1965; Vol. 8: 1966–1968; Vol. 9 onwards: Annual
Now published in April, August, and with a bound cumulation in December   25 cm

ARRANGEMENT: The main sequence is an alphabetical arrangement of subject headings. This is preceded by a Prefatory Note and a list of Periodical Abbreviations. There is no author index. The 1977 volume had 434 pages of index entries with between 30 and 50 entries a page. With about 20,000 entries a year, *Bibliographic Index* is probably the biggest current indexing service of bibliographies. The subject headings are arranged alphabetically with a limited amount of sub-division, usually geographical divisions. The headings, which include personal names, are quite specific. Strings of qualifying terms are kept to a minimum, while references to related terms are generously provided.

COVERAGE: '*Bibliographic Index* is a subject list of bibliographies published separately or appearing as parts of books, pamphlets, and periodicals. Selection is made from bibliographies which have fifty or more citations. The Index concentrates on titles in the Germanic and Romance languages.' (Prefatory Note). The existence of serial indexing and abstracting services is indicated under the appropriate subject headings. It claims that some 2400 periodicals are regularly examined for bibliographies. All subjects are covered. In 1977 for example, there were four bibliographies on Eschatology, nine on Religious Education, and one on Paul Tillich.

COMMENT: Most entries relate to the year in question, but entries from publications up to seven years old are not uncommon. There is about a six-month delay for the cumulated volume, two to three months for the others. The alphabetical arrangement, clear subject headings, good layout and frequent *see also* references make *Bibliographic Index* easy to use. The difficulty arises when its subject headings do not fit one's own description of the subject required – always a drawback with subject descriptors. To this extent it complements rather than supplants other classified lists. It is valuable, though, for its extensive coverage. *Bibliographic Index* only refers one to another bibliography or bibliographies. Further searching will still be necessary, and most searchers will be advised to try subject bibliographies first, and *Bibliographic Index* when other listings fail, or are out of date, or unknown.

Published by the H. W. Wilson Company, 950 University Avenue, Bronx, New York 10452, U.S.A.
ISSN 0006-1255

38 Bibliographie Annuelle de l'Histoire de France
Vol. 1– ; 1953–
Annual; no cumulations   24 cm

ARRANGEMENT: This is a full-scale bibliography arranged in a classified order. One major section in the classification, together with examples of sub-division, is:

Histoire Religieuse
  Catholicisme
    Les Missions Étrangères.

In the 1978 volume this major section had 1130 entries. After the bibliographical section and the preceding Plan de Classement, there is a detailed subject index covering some 160 pages and a substantial author index. Each entry in the main bibliographical section indicates the author(s), title and brief bibliographical details.

COVERAGE: The subject of this comprehensive bibliography is French history. Books and journal articles are covered, and a total of 10,225 items were listed in the 1978 volume. Material is largely of French origin.

COMMENT: This is an impressive bibliography with wide coverage, clearly arranged, well indexed and nicely produced. An essential tool for those concerned with French history. A two-year delay for articles to appear in the index seems common.

Published by the Centre National de la Recherche Scientifique, 15 Quai Anatole France, 75700 Paris, France ISSN 0067-6918

Bibliographie Internationale de l'Humanisme et de la Renaissance
Vol. 1– ; 1965–
Annual; no cumulations   22 cm

ARRANGEMENT: This massive work since Volume 9 (the latest is Volume 10) has appeared in two parts. The first part lists articles and books about anonymous works, or about people, of the renaissance period. The second part contains a bibliography arranged by subject of renaissance topics. There are indexes of proper names and subjects, as well as of the journals and collected works which have been noticed.

COVERAGE: The list of journals which is provided runs to well over 2500 titles, and there are books as well, all of which add up to more than 6000 citations on all aspects of the renaissance. The interest here, however, is particularly in religious studies. Under the heading Religion there were over 550 entries in Volume 10. The geographical spread is to most of Europe and America.

COMMENT: This is a mammoth undertaking, and is, for the most part, very well done. But the researcher should not rely upon it to keep up to date. There is currently a five-year delay between the year covered and the date of publication of the *Bibliographie*. Thus the volume for 1974 was published in 1979, and even then contained some older material. Currency has, in fact, been declining since the *Bibliographie* began.

Published on the recommendation of the Conseil International de la Philosophie et des Sciences Humaines, with the support of UNESCO.
Published for the Fédération Internationale des Sociétés et Instituts pour l'Étude de la Renaissance, by Éditions Aroz, 8 Rue Verdaine, 1200 Geneva, Switzerland
ISSN 0067-7000

40 **Bibliographie zur Symbolik, Ikonographie und Mythologie (BSIM)**
Internationales Referateorgan
Vol. 1–   ; 1968–
Annual; no cumulations, but cumulative index for Volumes 1–10   22.5 cm

ARRANGEMENT: Each volume contains one article dealing with some fundamental aspect of symbolism. This appears at the beginning, and is followed by reviews of Publications Relevant to Research as well as Instruction, compiled by an international team of scholars writing in English, French or German. Each entry should explain what the item being summarized says and 'if required, the particular perspective of the author and the actual state of investigation'. The reviews, usually quite short, are initialled and arranged in author sequence. They are numbered, and contain the minimum of bibliographical information. Each volume, of about 180 pages, has an author and an essential subject index.

Coverage: Both articles and books are included – there were 636 entries in the 1978 volume. How wide the coverage is there is no clear means of telling, since no list of periodicals has appeared. Selection seems to be left to the contributors.

Comment.: Although there is an entry for Religion in the subject index, the number of items listed under it is small. On the other hand there are many other entries which would interest a student of religious symbolism, of iconography or of mythology covering most of the world's religions. Currency is not good: the 1978 volume has material going back to 1974. The low-level bibliographical information may make it difficult for the inexperienced to find his or her way to the original article or book. The somewhat haphazard (or so it appears) means of collecting entries means that although both Eastern and Western Europe are satisfactorily covered, and the United States as well, there is little material gathered from outside those areas. Despite these hesitations, the *BSIM* provides an extremely useful service, albeit within a very narrow field.

Published by Verlag Valentin Koerner, Postfach 304, D-7570 Baden-Baden, Federal Republic of Germany
ISSN 0067-706X

Bibliographische Berichte / Bibliographical Bulletin
Vol. 1–   ; 1959–
Until Volume 19, for 1977, this was an annual publication. Semi-annual   24 cm

Arrangement: Each issue lists the bibliographies received by the Staatsbibliothek Preussischer Kulturbesitz. The bibliographies are arranged in broad subject fields, with sub-headings as necessary. Religion; Theology is a major heading with only two sub-headings, at least, as far as the list of contents is concerned. In practice additional sub-headings appear to be used where necessary. There is no index, but one is hardly required.

Coverage: The term 'bibliography' is widely interpreted,

and periodical indexes or published library catalogues have been included in this listing of any worthwhile bibliography of any size. A large number of the items included are in German, although many other languages can be found including, in recent volumes, the Slavonic languages.

COMMENT: About 110 items were included in the 1978 issues, the majority of them having been published in 1977, though there were a few from 1976 and a scattering from even earlier. This 'bibliography of bibliographies in religion' is extremely useful because it lists items not easily found through other tools, and draws attention to bibliographies hidden away in periodicals or multi-author works, though it does not seem to include the bibliographical features which appear on a regular basis as part of a periodical. In this it is unlike the *Bibliographic Index* (No. 37) which it complements, especially for European materials. Though the headings are in both English and German, introductory matter and notes are only in the latter language, which could be a handicap.

Published by Staatsbibliothek Preussischer Kulturbesitz, Vittorio Klostermann, Box 900601, 6 Frankfurt am Main 90, Federal Republic of Germany
ISSN 0006-1506

42 Bibliography of Asian Studies (BAS)

Vol. 1–   ; 1954–
Annual   25 cm

ARRANGEMENT: The main section of this work is the classified section which is arranged in broad geographical categories and then sub-divided by subject. One of the subject divisions is for Philosophy and Religion. Thus:

Japan
    Philosophy and Religion
        —Bibliography
        —Reference
    —Buddhism
    —Christianity
    —Confucianism

The actual sub-sections vary within the subject divisions from area to area. A detailed outline of the classification is given in the contents pages. Some entries are duplicated where more than one area or subject is covered, and some *see also* references are given. Concise bibliographical details are given in each entry with fuller details of the books analysed and the abbreviations used for journal titles provided with the prefatory matter. A list of periodical titles indexed is also given. The main bibliographical section is followed' by an author index. Reference from the index to the main section is by a key number which precedes the bibliographical entry. The entries are not annotated.

COVERAGE: 'The *BAS* aims to provide a comprehensive listing of publications in Western languages on East, South and Southeast Asia in the fields of history, the humanities and the social sciences.' (Preface). Monographs, journal articles, articles in Festschriften and commemorative volumes, government and international agency reports are covered. Each volume attempts to concentrate on publications of the year of the volume. In the 1975 volume, 133 books were analysed and some 510 journals. Together, these contributed to a total 17,775 entries, of which perhaps some 1000 were for religion.

COMMENT: For the most part, each annual volume covers items for that year, but there is a publication delay of some three years. *BAS* is straightforward and easy to use since entries covering religion are separately noted in each country or area. A thematic, non-regional approach is more difficult though. The lack of abstracts and annotations, together with the lack of translations, is regretted at times. The coverage, though, is impressive, and *BAS* is an essential work for those interested in Asia, Asian religions, or in Christian missionary studies.

Published by the Association for Asian Studies Inc., AAS Secretariat, 1 Lane Hall, University of Michigan, Ann Arbor, Michigan 48109, U.S.A.
ISSN 0067-7159

43   Bibliography of Bioethics
Vol. 1–   ; 1975–
Annual bound volume   28 cm

ARRANGEMENT: After the introduction and instructions for use, there are five main sections to the Bibliography: list of journals cited; bioethics thesaurus; subject entry section; title index; author index. Volume 3 has 348 pages. The subject entries (occupying 238 pages) are arranged in alphabetical order of subjects. The headings are chosen from the thesaurus, a carefully limited vocabulary, and are made up by one or two or more terms in combination. There are also many *see also* references to other terms. Under each subject heading the full bibliographical details of each book or periodical article are given, followed by a list of 10, 20 or more terms (descriptors) indicating the detailed subject matter of the item analysed.

COVERAGE: 'Bioethics can be defined as the systematic study of value questions which arise in the biomedical and behavioral fields'. Its interdisciplinary nature is seen in a selection of the major terms used in the thesaurus: medical ethics, health care, contraception, abortion, population, mental health therapies, human experimentation, artificial or transplanted organs, death and dying, biological warfare.
  Indexing is extended to books (in whole or part), journal or newspaper articles, law court decisions, legislative bills, audiovisual materials and unpublished documents.
  The editors say that Volume 3 has 1512 entries. About 450 periodical titles are listed. English-language materials only are cited – from North America, Great Britain and the Far East (if published in English).

COMMENT: In Volume 3 '70 were published in 1973, 215 in 1974, 1225 in 1975, and 2 in 1976'. Volume 1 covered mainly 1973, and Volume 2, 1974. Volume 3 was received in Edinburgh in June, 1978. Volume 1 was reviewed in the *Bulletin of the Association of British Theological and Philosophical Libraries*, New Series, No. 8 (March 1977) by A. V. Campbell, editor of the *Journal of Medical Ethics*: 'The comprehensiveness, originality, and sophistication of this bibliography justify its becoming the standard reference resource in this new and rapidly expanding field'. He compared it with the *Bibliography of Society, Ethics and the Life Sciences* (No. 45) of the Hastings Center, and the *Bioethics Digest* of Information Planning Associates, Rockville, Maryland, U.S.A., and concluded that the *Bibliography of Bioethics* would be the primary source of references for the serious researcher. It is probable that in this group of subjects the amount of material excluded by the editor's monoglot selection policy is slight. Each volume is substantially bound, and Volumes 2 and 3 very well printed, using large type sizes and a good variety of bold headings.

Compiled at the Center for Bioethics, Kennedy Institute, Georgetown University, Washington, D.C. 20057, U.S.A. Published by Gale Research Company, Book Tower, Detroit, Michigan 48226, U.S.A.

Bibliography of Philosophy / Bibliographie de la Philosophie
Vol. 1–   ; 1937–
Quarterly; Annual index   24.5 cm

ARRANGEMENT: Under these subject headings: (1) Philosophy in General; (2) Logic and Philosophy of Science; (3) Philosophical Psychology; (4) Aesthetics; (5) Ethics and Values; (6) Social Philosophy; (7) Culture and Education; (8) Religion; (9) History of Philosophy; (10) Reference Books and Miscellanea; and then in author order within the subject divisions. For all books the following information is provided: Author(s) or Editor(s); title and subtitle, preface, translator; place of publication, publisher, date; dimensions of book, pagination, 'series'. Indexes are published in the fourth issue of each year, indexed by author, title, and subject. There is also an index of quoted names, and an index of publishers (arranged by country).

COVERAGE: The bibliography covers books only, not periodicals. New books published for the first time are provided with abstracts (maximum 300 words). The length of each abstract generally indicates its importance. Reprints, re-editions, paperbacks, and translations do not receive an abstract, and are listed at the end of each section, or only in the fourth issue. Contributors come from all parts of the world (33 national centres are listed at the front of the bibliography), including the U.S.S.R., U.S.A., Australia, France, Great Britain. Abstracts are in one of the several languages – English, French, Spanish, German – and the names of the abstractors are listed. The aim of the bibliography is completeness of coverage, although this is dependent upon whether authors and/or publishers transmit information about their books to the national centre.

COMMENTS: The *Bibliography of Philosophy* appears to be a first-rate bibliographical tool for philosophy (and also some related subjects) both in the depth of its coverage, and the many areas of the world that it covers. The layout is impressive, as is the indexing itself. All possible ways of approaching an entry are thought of, even through the publisher. It is an excellent international bibliography, and a useful complement to the *Philosopher's Index*.

Published by the International Institute of Philosophy, Librairie Philosophique J. Vrin, 6 Place de la Sorbonne, 75005 Paris, France
ISSN 0006-1352

45 Bibliography of Society, Ethics and the Life Sciences
A selected and partially annotated bibliography
Vol. 1–   ; 1973–
Annual   28 cm

ARRANGEMENT: By broad subject headings, with much more specific sub-divisions. Within the sub-divisions arrangement is alphabetical by author, and there is an author index.

COVERAGE: All aspects of bioethics are included, and this necessarily takes in a great deal of material that is of little interest to anyone studying religion. There are, however, a number of headings for Ethics, and one specifically entitled Theological Ethics. Both books and articles are entered, and there is some coverage of report literature. The *Bibliography* aims to provide a basic reading list as well as a continuing information service. This combination of the two functions results in a certain lack of currency in some areas. The policy is to replace out-of-date citations with more up-to-date ones, as well as to add to the *Bibliography* as a whole. Entries are not numbered, but the 1979/80 edition contained approximately 2400.

COMMENT: The main value of the *Bibliography* is as an introduction to the subject, and the Preface gives the reader valuable advice on other bibliographies which might be of help, and on computer searching. As a fully comprehensive or retrospective bibliography its usefulness is limited by the policy of replacing out-of-date citations. It is not in the same class as the *Bibliography of Bioethics* (No. 43), but is a useful tool nonetheless.

Published by the Institute of Society, Ethics and the Life Sciences, 360 Broadway, Hastings-on-Hudson, New York 10706, U.S.A.
ISSN 0094-4813

Bibliotheca Celtica

A register of publications relating to Wales and the Celtic peoples and languages
Vol. 1–   ; 1909–
Annual; except for 1914–1952 which are covered by nine-cumulated volumes, and except for 1969–1970 and 1971–1972, each of which cover two years   21 cm

ARRANGEMENT: Each volume since 1929 is a classified listing (by the Library of Congress scheme) of items on all subjects. The latest volume has xxiii + 594 pages of which 28 cover religion. The arrangement under each subject sub-heading is alphabetically by author. Entries are not annotated. There is a list of periodicals indexed and an index of personal names.

COVERAGE: As stated in the sub-title, the geographical area covered is the Principality of Wales, and includes Ireland, Scotland, Man, Cornwall and Brittany. All subjects are included. The Religion section includes Church and pre-Christian history, and religious ideas within the Celtic cultures. Books, periodical articles and book reviews are covered. The 1971/72 volume has 264 entries under the heading Religion. About 400 periodicals are covered. Publications indexed are mainly in English or Welsh, though other European languages are represented.

COMMENT: The volume for 1971–1972 was published in 1976 and is the most recent. Books included were published in those two years. Presumably the same applies to the periodical articles, but dates of these are omitted, entries having only volume and page references. Selection is made from material received at the National Library of Wales. 'Celtic' is interpreted broadly, and in 1971–1972 includes the work of a Welsh preacher in London, and, under Mission, two Welsh, one Irish and four Scottish items. Its 'fringe' is likely to overlap other bibliographies, and its value in this context to lie in its specifically Welsh ecclesiastical coverage.

Published by Llyfrgell Genedlaethol Cymru, The National Library of Wales (and printed on its private press), Aberystwyth, Dyfed, Wales, U.K.

47   Bibliotheca Orientalis (BiOr)
Vol. 1–   ; 1943–
Six times a year   30 cm

ARRANGEMENT: Each issue contains a number of fairly long book reviews. There appears to be no particular method of arrangement for these. This section is followed by a brief News section, and a list of books received. There is no index.

COVERAGE: The *BiOr* appears to cover everything published concerning the Near East. Hebraica, Judaica, early Christian and Islamic items are all included, as well as much material on the archaeology, history, culture and language of the area. Books dominate the review section, but there are also entries for issues of periodicals devoted to a single theme, and Festschriften and conference proceedings are often analysed, and separate reviews provided for each paper. Books in most Western languages are covered, and the reviews are in the language of the reviewer – English, French and German being the most frequently used. Each issue contains 70–80 reviews.

COMMENT: Currency is poor. The issue for 1977 included a number of items from as far back as 1974, though the majority were from 1976. The arrangement of the items causes some frustration and much confusion, and the only way to trace religious material is by scanning the contents pages. It should be noted that the introductory material, headings and all other information are given in Dutch. This is a scholarly publication of considerable value, but in much need of improvement from the user's point of view.

Published by the Nederlands Instituut voor het Nabije Oosten, Noordeindsplein 4–6, Leiden, Netherlands
ISSN 0006-1913

Book List of the Society for Old Testament Study (BoL)
Vol. 1– ; 1946–
Annual; cumulations c. every ten years (but see under *Comment*)   21–22 cm

ARRANGEMENT: The latest issue is divided into ten rather than eleven (1974–1978) or twelve (1957–1973) sections. They are as follows: General; Archaeology and Epigraphy; History and Geography; Text and Versions; Exegesis and Modern Translations; Literary Criticism and Introductions; Law, Religion and Theology; the Life and Thought of the Surrounding Peoples; Apocrypha and Post-Biblical Studies; Philology and Grammar. The reductions have been brought about by the amalgamation of the Dead Sea Scrolls/Qumran studies with Apocrypha and Post-Biblical studies, and by denoting books suitable for inclusion in school libraries by an asterisk, in preference to listing them under Educational/School Textbooks, etc., in a special section. Each issue ends with a list of books received too late for notice, and an index of authors. No doubt reflecting the considerable growth of published material in the last few years, the size of each issue has risen gradually from under 100 pages ten years ago to over 150 pages today.

COVERAGE: The *Book List* does not include dissertations, but in addition to reviews of monographs, encyclopaedias, dictionaries, colloquia, Festschriften etc. are included. Although the *Book List* depends upon the supply of review copies, its stature is such that this does not present any major problem: no significant omissions have been noted. No list of publishers is appended, but the coverage is international.

COMMENT: Since its inception the *Book List* has been the responsibility of only four editors – Professors Rowley, Anderson, Ackroyd and Whybray – which goes some way to explaining its continuity and its success. The academic standing of the editors has helped to guarantee the standard of reviewing, and distinguished contributors abound. Reviews tend to be short – on average, a third of a page – and the latest issue contains approximately four hundred. Most of the books looked at were 1977 or 1978 publications, though a few stragglers have thrust themselves in from 1976, and one or two from 1979 have crept forward. The *Book List* is a most valuable guide to the literature, easy to use and reliable. Its principal limitation arises from the discipline of space, so that some reviews suffer from being excessively condensed, and others are telegrammatic to the point of enigma. It should be noted that cumulations have been published as follows: *Eleven Years of Bible Bibliography*, edited by H. H. Rowley (The Falcon's Wing Press, 1957); *A Decade of Bible Bibliography*, edited by G. W. Anderson (Basil Blackwell, 1967); *Bible Bibliography 1967–1973: Old Testament*, edited by Peter R. Ackroyd (Basil Blackwell, 1974). These are little more than compilations of the individual lists.

Published by The Editor, S.O.T.S. Book List, Department of Theology, University of Hull, Cottingham Road, Hull HU6 7RX, U.K.

9   Book Reviews of the Month (BRM)

An index to reviews appearing in selected theological journals
Vol. 1–   ; 1962–
Monthly   21.5 cm

ARRANGEMENT: This is by the Dewey Decimal class number, enhanced by the provision of verbal descriptors for each class number, and supplemented by an author index. Entries in the author index refer back to the DDC numbers, so particular entries may take a short time to trace, since references are not unique identifiers.

COVERAGE: Any book which could be classed in the DDC 200 (i.e. anything to do with religion) class is included. There are also sections for philosophy, geography, history, the social sciences and literature, as well as occasional items from other groups such as archaeology, linguistics and so on. At present about one hundred journals are scanned for reviews, and they cover books in the main Western languages.

COMMENT: All the reviews included in the March 1979 issue were published in journals published either that year, or the year before – speed of information is one of the objects of this service. The date of publication of the books noticed, however, can be much earlier – items from 1977 abound, and there were some from 1976 as well. But this is a reflection on the review editors of the journals, rather than on *BRM* itself. This is a very useful tool, and although those unfamiliar with DDC may find it a little difficult to use at first, there is an ample list of subject headings to help overcome this problem. Entries give only author, title, publisher and date, with a reference to the journals, most of them fairly readily available, where the review may be found. Compared with *Religious Studies Review* (No. 140), however, the main disadvantage is that the user has to move on somewhere else.

Published by Fleming Library, Southwestern Baptist Theological Seminary, Fort Worth, Texas 76122, U.S.A.
ISSN 0006-7362

50 British Archaeological Abstracts
Vol. 1– ; 1967–
Semi-annual   20 cm

ARRANGEMENT: A classified approach is adopted with the abstracts arranged in broad subject groups. The general order is chronological with a standard set of sub-divisions to each period. A table is provided in the prefatory matter to make the plan clear. Each abstract is signed and covers a brief paragraph. Essential bibliographical details are provided. Some twenty to thirty abstracts of interest to religious studies occur per issue. The headings: Pre-Christian/Pagan, and Christian Monuments – Buildings and Sites cover most of these. Author and subject indexes to each issue are provided.

COVERAGE: 124 British and some 68 foreign journals are consulted and the actual issues indexed are listed. The subject matter is British archaeology. It is the previous year's journals that are generally covered.

COMMENTS: Of interest to those studying the early history of Christianity in Britain or the history of particular buildings or localities.

Published by the Council for British Archaeology, 112 Kennington Road, London SE11 6RE, U.K.
ISSN 0007-0270

51 British Education Index (BEI)
Vol. 1– ; 1954–
Some of the earlier volumes cover more than one year.
Quarterly; annual cumulation in the last issue   30 cm

ARRANGEMENT: The main section is the Subject List of Articles which gives full citations of the articles indexed: author, title of article, title of periodical in an abbreviated form, the number of pages, the issue number or date of the periodical in which it was published. Entries are arranged under subject headings representing the subject treated, and each subject heading is given a running citation number. The 1977 volume had headings for Theology, Religion, Religious Development, Religious Education, Moral Education and Church of England. Some of these were further sub-divided. The Subject Index contains terms which express the contents of the articles indexed. Each entry in the Subject Index refers to one or more citation numbers which can be found in the Subject List of Articles. The Author Index contains full citations of articles under the name of author. A List of Titles of Periodicals and Publishers gives information on the frequency, ISSN, name and full address of each periodical indexed. There are prefatory notes on how to use the index and a list of the periodicals indexed.

COVERAGE: '*British Education Index* aims to list and analyse the subject content of all articles of permanent educational interest which have appeared in a wide range of English language periodicals published or distributed in the British Isles.' (Preface). One hundred and seventy five periodicals are currently indexed, though few of a specialist religious nature. The 1977 volume had 2518 subject headings covering some 3500 articles. About 20 of these were on religion.

COMMENT: The quarterly issues appear promptly although the annual cumulation takes six months or more to appear. The layout and straightforward arrangement of heading make this an easy index to use, but the relatively small number of religious items that the mainstream British education journals seem to generate, combined with the fact that educational items in specially religious journals are not indexed, make this an item of value only to those interested in secular religious education or doing a comprehensive literature search on religious education in general.

See also *Current Index to Journals in Education* (No. 76), and *Education Index* (No. 81).

Published by the British Library, Bibliographic Services Division, Store Street, London WC1E 7DG, U.K.
ISSN 0007-0637

52   British Humanities Index (BHI)

Vol. 1–   ; 1962–
Supersedes *Subject Index to Periodicals*, 1915–1922; 1926–1961.
Quarterly; annual cumulations   30 cm

ARRANGEMENT: *BHI* is arranged alphabetically by subject headings. The headings are specific, with references from broader and related subjects where relevant. The index entries themselves are brief, with title of article, author(s), journal title, volume number (date and year), pagination, and a note of any illustrations and references. An index of the authors indexed is included in the annual cumulation only. There is a list of the journals indexed at the front of every issue. The annual volume contains about 580 pages of the subject index and about 230 pages of the author index. There are between 50 and 60 index entries per page excluding cross-references.

COVERAGE: Subject coverage is the humanities and social sciences. The sources covered are solely journals, magazines and a few national newspapers. About 370 titles are indexed, of which there are 18 specialist religious journals. All but one are British publications.

COMMENT: *BHI* appears about two months after the end of the quarterly indexing period, and all but a few of the entries relate to that quarterly period. The annual volumes appear five to six months after the end of the year.

The straightforward alphabetical arrangement of subject headings is easy to follow and there is a liberal supply of references to related headings and preferred terms, e.g. Ethics *related heading* Sin. Complex subjects are arranged by the chain indexing system with specific subject terms filing before more general ones: such detailed headings usefully identify the content of cryptic article headings.

BHI is probably the most widely used indexing journal in British libraries. Although generalist in subject coverage it contains quite specialized items. It is particularly useful for picking up articles on religious topics from journals and magazines not normally covered by specialist religious abstracting and indexing tools, e.g. *The Daily Telegraph*, *The Spectator*, *German Life and Letters*. *BHI* is also useful for covering fringe subject fields such as archaeology, literature, music, art and regional studies.

Published by the Library Association, 7 Ridgmount Street, London WC1E 7AE, U.K.
ISSN 007-0815

53 British National Bibliography (BNB)

A subject catalogue of new British books received by the Copyright Receipt Office of the British Library, arranged according to the Dewey Decimal Classification and catalogued according to the British text of the Anglo-American Cataloguing Rules, with a full author and title index, a subject index, and a list of publishers.
Vol. 1–   ; 1950–.
Weekly;   four-monthly,   annual   and   multi-annual cumulations   30 cm

ARRANGEMENT: The Weekly Lists are arranged in classified order: each entry is classified by the current edition of the Dewey Decimal Classification scheme and arranged in the order of the classification numbers. Some entries appear under two or more numbers. Each weekly issue has an author and title index. The last Weekly List for each month has a cumulated author and title index for that month and a subject index for the month.

The Interim Cumulations cover January–April and May–August each year, and cumulate the classified sequences, the author and title indexes, and the subject indexes for the four-month period. They also have a list of publishers, with their addresses, for all items listed (except where publisher's details are included with the individual entries).

The Annual Volumes cumulate, at present, the classified arrangement in one volume, and the author and title indexes, the subject indexes, and the list of publishers for the year in the second volume.

Cumulated Subject Catalogues in two to three volumes, and Cumulated Indexes in one volume each, have been produced for 1950–1954 (1951–1954 in the case of the Subject Catalogue), 1955–1959, 1960–1964, 1965–1967 and 1968–1970. The former cumulates the classified sequences for the years covered, and the latter cumulate the author, title and subject index sections of the annual volumes in question. The Cumulated Index volumes also cumulate the list of publishers. The Cumulated Index for 1971–1973 contains author, title and publisher indexes only, not a subject index.

The fullest entry occurs in the classified arrangement where a full catalogue entry is given following the classification number and subject heading. Author, title, sub-titles, publisher, date, pagination, size, ISBN, ISSN and BNB number are also given together with any other useful bibliographical information such as date of original or previous editions, tables, or illustrative material. In addition to the subject heading for the classification number, each entry is given an extended feature-heading to cover the book's subject matter and to indicate any special features such as: Illustrations, Facsimile, Statistics, or other relevant information, e.g. Juvenile Literature, Reviews of Research, German Text. The author and title indexes include publisher, price, class number, ISBN and BNB number. The subject indexing is full and covers feature headings. An example is:

Southwell (Diocese). Church of England—*Directories* 283.42524.

Most entries covering religious subjects will be arranged in Class 200, the Dewey number for Religion, though many other entries for religious subjects, especially if related to other subjects, will be found in other parts of the classification. Access to these can be made through the subject indexes.

COVERAGE: As indicated in the subtitle, *BNB* lists all new British books received by the Copyright Receipt Office of the British Library, and therefore serves as a national bibliography. In addition to books and pamphlets, the first issues of periodicals, editions of annuals, and many government publications are included. The Weekly Lists also contain entries derived from advance information supplied by publishers. In 1978, *BNB* listed 40,671 items, which was a little larger than the 38,766 items listed in Whitaker's *Cumulated Book List*, the leading trade listing of books published during the year. *BNB* listed 1169 new titles in class 200 in 1978. Currency is very good, most items appearing within a few weeks after publication, and advance information being provided prior to publication for many others. Occasional older publications of a year or more earlier do occur and are due to late receipt at the Copyright Office.

COMMENT: Authoritative, detailed and comprehensive, *BNB* is the standard bibliography for British libraries. It is an essential starting point for any search for British material published since 1950. Although *BNB* covers all subjects, the detailed classification and subject indexing make for relatively easy searching. The cumulations are helpful. *BNB* entries are available in card form, and on computer file through BLAISE (British Library Automated Information Service).

Published by The British Library, Bibliographic Services Division, Store Street, London WC1E 7DG, U.K. ISSN 0007-1544

4 Buddhist Text Information (BTI)
Vol. 1– ; 1974–
Quarterly; cumulative index in the December issue
28 cm

ARRANGEMENT: This is by 'basic texts, with Romanized titles ... and brief identification. Entries are numbered consecutively in each issue'. There is a cumulated index to titles, and a name index to cover authors, editors, translators and so on published each year.

COVERAGE: Very broadly, anything connected with Buddhism. Coverage is determined almost entirely by the contributors, who submit information to the Institute for the Advanced Study of World Religions. The information comes from most Western countries as well as from some Oriental centres.

COMMENT: The *BTI* aims to alert researchers to work in progress and editions in the press, as well as to bring material already published to their attention. The text abounds in Sanskrit, Chinese and Japanese characters, which makes the *BTI* very difficult to use unless the reader is well acquainted with the language(s) he is concerned with. Each entry gives the text being worked upon, the publication details if any, the translator, editor and, sometimes, affiliation. References are not always easy to disentangle, but they are fairly extensively coded to indicate the type of work being done, whether, for instance, it is a catalogue, a glossary, whether it contains pictorial data, and so on. Many of the documents mentioned are unpublished, but may be acquired from the I.A.S.W.R. on microfiche, or in xerographic format, for a very low price. This is a rare example of an information service backed up by a document delivery service.

Published by the Institute for the Advanced Study of World Religions, Melville Memorial Library, State University of New York at Stony Brook, Stony Brook, New York 11794, U.S.A.
ISSN 0360-6112

55   Bulletin d'Arabe Chrétien
Vol. 1–   ; 1976–
Three times a year (but see *Comment*)   20.5 cm

ARRANGEMENT: The second issue contains a section (pages 29–40) headed Publications Récentes, which is subdivided into Livres, Articles, Thèses et Mémoires Polycopies, Travaux sous Presse, and Abstracts. Within each section arrangement is alphabetical by author, but as the number of entries is small this, and the lack of an author index, do not present problems.

COVERAGE: The scope is meant to be all items concerning Christian Arabs, or the Christian world in an Arab context. As the first issue of the *Bulletin* pointed out, such material is often to be found scattered throughout journals which deal with Armenian, Syriac, Coptic or Georgian studies, and is therefore difficult to locate by scholars interested in Arab Christianity. The *Bulletin's* aim is to bring all this material together in regular bibliographies, and also to provide information both on individual scholars in the field, and on work in progress. Coverage of the proposed bibliography is largely confined to periodicals, but the language spread is considerable. In the first issue a provisional list of 136 Roman alphabet and 18 Arabic journals was provided, and the next issue increased the total to 192, each with the name of the indexer attached. These were to be scanned for relevant items. The bibliographical apparatus so far published covers books, journals and theses. Brief notes, with references to reviews, were provided for 45 books in the third issue, which appeared in 1977. There were short abstracts of, or notes on, 55 articles, many of which appeared in specialized journals not readily available in the majority of libraries. The third issue also included a bibliography of four authors working in the field.

COMMENT: The *Bulletin* is rather more of an aspiration than an actuality. The editor expressed the hope that a *Bibliographie d'Arabe Chrétien* for 1960–1969 would appear in 1978, for 1950–1959 in 1979, and 1940–1949 in 1979. The bibliography for 1970–1979 would then appear in 1981, that for 1980 would be prepared for the 1982 volume, and then so on annually. The retrospective bibliographies, however, have yet to appear. If the *Bulletin* succeeds it will provide a very useful service for a highly specialized, if somewhat limited, audience. Non-specialist users are likely to be confused by the one-letter-per-word type of abbreviation for journal titles – some of them very obscure. So far (and no issue for 1978 had been received by the end of 1979) production has been by offset litho, and costs have been kept very low.

Published by David D. Bundy, Vandenbemptlaan 3, 3030-Harlevee, Belgium

56 **Bulletin de la Société de L'Histoire du Protestantisme Français (BSHPF)**
Vol. 1–   ; 1853–
Quarterly; Cumulative indexes for 1852–1902; 1902–1927; 1928–1940   24 cm

ARRANGEMENT: Each issue contains scholarly articles, edited texts of historical documents, obituaries, news of the Society's activities, and Chronique Littéraire et Comptes Rendus. Each volume has about 600 pages, of which the Chronique occupies about 80. This comprises a book review section, not systematically arranged, followed by Revues – abstracts of periodical articles. The text is all in French.

COVERAGE: The *Bulletin* is confined to the history of Protestant Christianity in France, national and local, but this can include topics from alchemy to freemasonry, and names from Calvin to Rousseau and Voltaire. The number of periodical articles abstracted is very small, mostly from local French sources. Books and conference reports from French and other European sources are mostly substantial and all signed.

COMMENT: Books are usually reviewed within one or two years of publication, though some are delayed much longer. It is not an easily consulted source of information, but offers great detail for the serious inquirer into French Protestant history.

Published with the support of the Centre National de la Recherche Scientifique, by the Société de l'Histoire du

Protestantisme Français, 54 Rue des Saint-Pères, 75007 Paris
7ᶜ, France
ISSN 0037-9050

7 **Bulletin de Théologie Ancienne et Médiévale /
Bulletin of Ancient and Medieval Christian
Literature (BThAM)**

Vol. 1–   : 1933–

The *BThAM* originally appeared as separately paginated
sections of the *Recherches de Théologie Ancienne et Médiévale*, the
first volume of the *Bulletin* covering the years from 1929,
when the *Recherches* began, to 1932. From Volume 4
(1941–1945) onwards, however, it has appeared as a separate
publication, each annual fascicule consisting of about 120
pages going to make up a single volume covering several
years. So Volume 11 took in the years 1970–1975, and the
latest volume, 12, began to appear in mid-1977 for the years
from 1976. Fascicule 3 of Volume 12 was published in
mid-1979 for January–December 1978.

Annual; no cumulations   25.5 cm

ARRANGEMENT: Signed abstracts are provided for well over
2250 books, articles and dissertations in a complete volume,
appearing at the rate of approximately 350 entries a year.
They are listed in chronological order of the period they
cover. The centuries are marked, not always very distinctly,
in the margins, but there are no other divisions of the list.
Full indexes are published only when the volume is
complete, but an index of names is provided on the paper
covers of the individual fascicules. In the complete volume
there are three indexes – of names, of theological topics,
and of manuscripts.

COVERAGE: The words 'ancient and medieval' in the title are
interpreted generously. The *BThAM* extends from New
Testament times to the end of the sixteenth century in its
range of interest. 'Literature' is also widely interpreted, and
it is worth consulting the *BThAM* for anything on early and
medieval Christianity, except Scripture. Most of the books
and periodicals abstracted are Western European or North

American, though that might be expected, given the nature of the subject. No list of periodicals scanned has, apparently, been published, which makes the extent of the coverage difficult to judge.

COMMENT: There is nothing quite like the *BThAM*, and one has to accept that it fills a very real gap, while wishing that the gap might be filled more efficiently. Currency is bad, even allowing for the problem, mentioned above, of having to wait so long for the indexes. Without the indexes the usefulness of the *BThAM* is severely curtailed. When the indexes eventually arrive, however, they are excellent, especially that of theological topics, which is closely sub-divided by subject, and by period. The *BThAM* can be strongly recommended to any French-reading researcher – all the abstracts are in that language – so long as he is interested in retrospective bibliography and not in a 'current awareness' service.

Published by Recherches de Théologie Ancienne et Médiévale, Abbaye du Mont César, 202 Mechelse Straat, B-3000 Louvain, Belgium
ISSN 0007-442X

58   Bulletin of Dr. Williams's Library

Vol. 66–   ; 1961–
Supplements the printed catalogues of accessions of the Library covering 1900–1950, 1951–1960 and 1961–1970.
Annual

ARRANGEMENT: The *Bulletin* has seven preliminary pages of Library and Dr. Williams's Trust notes and news. The List of Accessions occupies the rest of its 26 pages. The List of Accessions [October 1977 – September 1978] runs in classified subject order, preceded by an outline of subjects. It is not annotated and has no index.

COVERAGE: The subjects included reflect the areas in which the Library specializes: theology, history of religion, philosophy, and ecclesiastical history, especially of English Nonconformity and the Byzantine world. It includes books, dissertations, offprints and selected periodicals mainly in English, but with some French, German, Dutch, and Latin.

COMMENT: The majority of items listed were published within the previous twelve months, with some items of all years from the previous decade. Its value is dependent on limited purchasing ability of an independent institution's endowment, subscriptions and gifts.

Published by Dr. Williams's Trust, 14 Gordon Square, London WC1H 0AG, U.K.

Bulletin of Medieval Canon Law (BMCL)
Vol. 1– ; 1971–

The Institue of Medieval Canon Law, which publishes this work, was established in 1955, and began producing a Select Bibliography in the pages of *Traditio* (New York, Fordham University Press) from the following year. The section devoted to the Institute grew from 20 pages in 1955 to 77 pages by 1970, at which point it was decided to establish a separate annual publication.

Annual; no cumulations   25 cm

ARRANGEMENT: *BMCL* takes the usual form for a learned journal, a group of scholarly communications followed by a bibliography which occupies about half the 110 or so pages. There is also a list of microfilms and photostats acquired by the Institute. Some of the articles are themselves bibliographical, and a regular – though not invariable – feature has been a list of books and articles on councils and synods to supplement J. T. Sawicki's *Bibliographia Synodorum Particularium* (Rome, 1967).

COVERAGE: In addition to the obvious entries for texts and individual canonists, the sixteen sections into which the Select Bibliography is broken down include headings such as Pope, Papacy, Curia; Councils and Synods; Ecclesiology, Sacerdotium and Regnum, Political Theory; Monasticism and Religious Orders; Universities and Other Centres of Learning. Both books and periodical articles are entered, the contents of Festschriften and even encyclopaedias are itemized, and reviews of works listed earlier are cited. There is no list of periodicals, but coverage seems fairly wide, granted that outside Western Europe and the Americas interest in medieval Canon Law is not very great. There is an index of names – a subject index is scarcely necessary, given the detailed break-down of the various sections.

COMMENT: This is a very thorough bibliography, both for the history of Canon Law in general, and for the history of the councils of the Church in particular. The currency is reasonable. Most of the citations in the 1978 issue were of books and articles published either in 1976 or 1977, though there were some from earlier years. However, the 1978 volume did not appear until half-way through 1979. Bibliographical information is just about adequate, and occasionally the compilers provide brief annotations, usually, it would seem, to explain the inclusion of an item. The bibliographic section of the *BMCL*, although it makes no claim to be exhaustive and is of a wider scope than that contained in the *Annuarium Historiae Conciliorum* (No. 17) compares very favourably with that of the latter publication – and is considerably cheaper to acquire.

Published by the Institute of Medieval Canon Law, School of Law (Boalt Hall), University of California, Berkeley, California 94720, U.S.A.

60 The Bulletin of the Scottish Institute of Missionary Studies
No. 1– ; 1967–
Irregular; no cumulations   25 cm

ARRANGEMENT: In some years of its existence, the Institute has published one issue comprising articles, notes and information on source materials and another comprising the Survey of Current Missionary Literature. There have been ten Surveys from 1969–1978. Number 20 (1976) has 112 pages. The survey has a systematic arrangement: the first half by subject (which are cross-referenced to the second half), and the second half by geographical region or territory (alphabetically).

COVERAGE: The Survey covers Christian mission in its widest sense: relationship to other world religions; relationship to environment, society and development; forms of ministry; catechesis and pastoralia. It is a detailed *book*-reviewing service, the reviews ranging from brief annotations to substantial critical assessments by appropriate reviewers. All are signed. Books on Roman Catholic missions appear to be outnumbered by those on Protestant work. Number 20 (1976) has 138 entries. The books reviewed are in English, French, German, Norwegian, etc.

COMMENT: In the 1976 edition approximately half the entries were published within the previous two years. Others date from three to ten years previously. But the 1976 edition was not received till May 1978. Further material is apparently available, but the Institute has had financial difficulties in having it published. The Survey is complementary to the Bibliography on World Mission and Evangelism (No. 102) in the *International Review of Mission*, which includes periodicals and reports as well as books, but is, for most entries, annotated. It shares the same editor.

Published by the Scottish Institute of Missionary Studies, Department of Religious Studies, University of Aberdeen, Kings College, Aberdeen AB9 2UB, Scotland, U.K.

Bulletin Signalétique 527: Histoire et Sciences des Religions (BSig.SR)
Vol. 1– ; 1947–
Quarterly; annual index   29.5 cm

ARRANGEMENT: Since its inception in 1947 the *Bulletin Signalétique* has spawned an increasing number of fascicules to cover ever smaller areas of research. At first the 'sciences of religion' were associated with philosophy and the 'sciences humaines', but the 'sciences religieuses' have had their own, independent section since 1970. The bibliography is organized into nine main divisions:

'Sciences des Religions'; 'Religions de l'Antiquité'; Israel; Christianity; Exegesis and Biblical Criticism; Islam; the Religions of Africa; the Religions of America, of the Arctic and of Oceania; the Religions of Asia. Each of these divisions is provided with its own index, and there are annual indexes, supplied in a separate fascicule, of authors, 'concepts' and of the periodicals scanned. The entries, which are numbered consecutively throughout each volume, give a bibliographical reference together with short abstract which, the compilers stress, is in no way a critical notice. In 1979 there were 8870 entries.

COVERAGE: The annual list of periodicals publishes the titles only of those journals from which a citation has been made in the past year – and, indeed, notes beside each one the numbers of the citations, which might be of value when trying to assess the worth, for a theological library, of particular publications. The list contains some 1200 titles, gathered from all over the world, but with a strong European–North American bias. The introduction points out that articles in English, French, German, Spanish, Italian, Portuguese and Latin are cited in the original language. Other languages are translated into French, and, of course all the abstracts likewise are in French. The intention is to cover the entire world in the selection of journals, the acts of conferences and colloquia, collections of essays, reports and French theses.

COMMENT: The entire *Bulletin Signalétique* is such a massive undertaking that it seems a pity some of the blanket-coverage it appears to give to other subjects does not rub off on to religion in Section 527. One of the major problems in the bibliography of religion is that articles of interest to students of the subject appear in unexpected places. Most of the journals listed in the *BSig.SR*, however, are fairly predictable philosophical and religious publications, and there does not seem to be as much representation of non-European and American periodicals as one might have expected. The preparation of separate indexes for the nine main subject fields seems a little unnecessary, and perhaps unwieldy for someone not wholly familiar with the subject being researched. Such problems, however, should be solved by recourse to the contents table, which is eminently thorough (the heading for Christianity alone has over 50 sub-divisions). To balance the criticisms, one ought to add that the currency is excellent, and the value of an indexing service which provides abstracts is enormous.

Published by Centre de Documentation Sciences Humaines, 54 Boulevard Raspail, BP 140, 75260 Paris Cedex 06, France ISSN 0180-9296

Byzantinische Zeitschrift (ByZ)
Vol. 1–   ; 1892–
Semi-annual   24 cm

ARRANGEMENT: Each issue contains scholarly articles, book reviews and a bibliographical section. The 1978 volume has 591 pages, of which 94 are occupied by book reviews and 387 by the Bibliographie. The Bibliographie is laid out in a very thorough systematic subject sequence. Abstracts, some lengthy, are given for about half the entries. All entries are identified by the initials of the contributor. Titles in less known languages, e.g. Rumanian, have German translations added. Authors of items included are indexed in the author index of the annual volume.

COVERAGE: The Eastern Roman Empire (A.D. 325–1453) centred on Byzantium: its history, archaeology, art, architecture, literature, linguistics, theology and ecclesiastical history. The most relevant headings are: 4.A. Theologische Literatur; 4.B. Apokryphen; 4.C. Hagiographie; 4.D. Dogmatik. Liturgik; 5.C. Religions- und Kirchengeschichte; 5.D. Mönchthum; 7.C. Ikonographie. Symbolik. Technik. Books, theses, book reviews and periodical articles, in many European and other languages, are included. The 1978 volume has an estimated 4000 entries.

COMMENT: A very high proportion of entries are included within two years of publication. Even a slight acquaintance with German allows this guide to be profitably used. It is excellent in its inclusiveness, subject arrangement, currency and indexing by author. It would be helpful if the scheme of subject arrangement given in volume 43 (1950) page 51 were repeated each time.

Published by C.H. Beck'sche Verlagsbuchhandlung, Wilhelmstrasse 9, Abholfach, D-8000 München 40, Federal Republic of Germany
ISSN 0007-7704

63   Byzantinoslavica (BySl)
Revue internationale des études byzantines
Vol. 1–   ; 1929–
Semi-annual   24 cm

ARRANGEMENT: Each issue contains scholarly articles and book reviews in French, Russian, German or English, and a bibliographical section. Each volume of about 300 pages has about 50 pages of book reviews and 150 of bibliography. The *Bibliographie* is arranged in a systematic subject sequence with abstracts or short reviews. The abstractors are identified by initials. Some but not all Russian titles have translations added.

COVERAGE: The Eastern Roman Empire centred on Byzantium: its history, archaeology, art, architecture, literature, linguistics, theology and ecclesiastical history. The most relevant headings are: V.C. Histoire de l'église, histoire des religions; VIII.B. Littérature théologique; VIII.C. Dogmatique, liturgie; VIII.D. Hagiographie; VIII.E. Apocryphes.
  Books, theses, book reviews and periodical articles are included. Languages include Russian, French, Greek, German, English and other European languages. The 1977 volume has an estimated 2000 entries.

COMMENT: Most entries relate to publications of the two previous years. Its subject arrangement is useful, and it is up to date, but far less inclusive than the *Bibliographie* of the *Byzantinische Zeitschrift* (No.62). The East European outlook of this periodical may provide a useful comparison with the corresponding German and Belgian guides.

Published by Editions Academia, Vodičkova 40, 112 29 Praha, Czechoslovakia, and obtainable through John Benjamins B.V., Periodical Trade, Amsteldijk 44, Amsterdam, Netherlands
ISSN 0007-7712

4   **Byzantion (Byz)**
Revue internationale des études byzantines
Vol. 1–   ; 1924–
Semi-annual;   Cumulated   index   to   Volumes   1–30 (1924–1960)   23 cm

ARRANGEMENT: Each volume (of 500–600 pages) contains scholarly articles, editions of original texts, book reviews and Notices Bibliographiques (27 pages in 1976). The Notices are published in one or both issues each year, giving abstracts or short reviews of books or articles arranged in alphabetical order of the original author's name. The abstractors are identified by initials.

COVERAGE: The Eastern Roman Empire centred on Byzantium: its history, archaeology, art, architecture, literature, linguistics, theology, and ecclesiastical history. Books and periodical articles are noted. The 1976 volume has about 60 abstracts, from works in French, German, English, Greek, Arabic, Russian.

COMMENT: Most items were published within two years of listing. There is no quick way of finding items on a particular subject. It cannot compare in scale or subject arrangement with the *Bibliographie* of the *Byzantinische Zeitschrift* (No.62).

Published with the support of the Ministère de l'Éducation Nationale et de la Culture Française et de la Fondation Universitaire de Belgique, by Fondation Byzantine, Boulevard de l'Empereur, 4, B-1000 Brussels, Belgium and obtainable through Éditions Universa, 24 Rue Hoender, B-9200 Wetteren, Belgium

65   Calvin Theological Journal (CTJ)
Vol. 1–   ; 1966–
Semi-annual; no cumulations   22.5 cm

ARRANGEMENT: The *Calvin Theological Journal* publishes an annual Calvin Bibliography in one of its semi-annual issues. It appears at the end of the articles section and before the book review section. The bibliography examined was that for 1979 and it extended over 27 pages of the issue. The remainder of the issue was devoted to two articles and book reviews. The bibliography is divided into seven sections: Bibliographies, Calvin's Works, Calvin's Life and Work, Calvin's Theology, Calvin's Aesthetic, Social-Ethical and Political Views, Calvin's Influence and Calvinism. Each section is further sub-divided as necessary, e.g. the Theology section is sub-divided as follows: General, Doctrine of God, Doctrine of Man, Doctrine of Christ and Salvation, Doctrine of Church and Sacraments. Within each section the entries are arranged alphabetically by author with the exception of the section entitled Calvin's Works where the entries are arranged alphabetically by title.

COVERAGE: The subjects covered therefore are all the different aspects of Calvin's life and work. A wide range of material is included in the bibliography: books, periodical articles, articles/chapters from books, dissertations, theses and articles from encyclopaedias and dictionaries. Some 30 entries are included and each has full bibliographical details, although there are no annotations. While much of the material is of American and British origin, there is a good coverage of material from other countries throughout the world. For the purposes of the bibliography, the closest English equivalents have been substituted for some of the non-English characters.

COMMENT: A considerable amount of current material is included, but a large proportion of the bibliography is retrospective. The value of the bibliography lies in its comprehensive nature as it appears to be definitive within the specialist field covered.

Published by the Calvin Theological Seminary, 3233 Burton Street, S.E., Grand Rapids, Michigan 49506, U.S.A. ISSN 0008-1975

6 Canon Law Abstracts (CLA)

A half-yearly review of periodical literature in Canon Law
Vol. 1– ; 1959–
Semi-annual; no cumulations   22 cm

ARRANGEMENT: The format has remained substantially unaltered for a number of years. The only change is a minor one, dividing the opening general and historical section into two. The rest of each issue is taken up with the *Code of Canon Law*, book by book, and canon by canon.

COVERAGE: The only subject covered is (Roman Catholic) Canon Law. It is considered historically, generally, and in terms of current applications and trends. The abstracting is from periodicals only. Each issue usually contains a small list of books received by the editor, but this book list is the sole intrusion of non-periodical material in this journal. Over the last ten years the number of periodicals regularly abstracted has risen gradually from 67 to 81, all of them Roman Catholic. The coverage is world wide. Much of the work of abstracting is done by members of the Canon Law Society of Great Britain and Ireland, scattered around the world.

COMMENT: The delay between the first appearance of an article, and the publication of an abstract in *CLA* is never less than six months, is quite frequently twelve months and occasionally, if an issue of a particular periodical is itself late in arriving, may be as much as eighteen months. *CLA* is very much a working tool, compiled by canon lawyers for canon lawyers. There are no concessions of any kind to those unfamiliar with the *Code*. No indexes have ever been published. All abstracts are in English, and the contributors are named. Over the last ten years the length of individual issues has varied slightly, but between 75 and 100 pages is normal, while the entries themselves vary in length from a few lines to a page and a half. Its limitations notwithstanding, CLA has many distinguished contributors, is inexpensive, and has no English language rival.

Published by The CLA Business Manager, Tollerton Hall, Nottingham, U.K.

67 Carmelus

Commentarii ab Instituto Carmelitano editi
Vol. 1–   ; 1954–
Semi-annual   23.5 cm

ARRANGEMENT: Each issue carries a number of scholarly articles on various aspects of the Carmelite Order, and in the second issue of each volume there is a bibliography arranged by 13 broad subject headings, with sub-heads as necessary. There is also an author and subject index.

COVERAGE: All aspects of the Carmelites are covered, the history and the liturgy of the Order, and works by, as well as works about, individual members. There are strong sections on sociology, education and psychology. Books, theses and journal articles are all included, with adequate bibliographical information. No list of periodicals scanned has been published, but the range is wide.

COMMENT: This is an excellent bibliographical tool for the study of this Order. Arrangement is clear, and easy to follow, although all headings and introductory material are in Italian, which may prove a disadvantage to some users. Currency varies considerably: the 1978 volume contained entries from 1970 to 1977, the earlier ones being for the most part monographs.

Published by the Institutum Carmelitanum, via Sforza Paltavicini 10, 00193 Roma, Italy
ISSN 0008-6673

Catholic Historical Review (CHR)

Official organ of the American Catholic Historical Association
Vol. 1–   ; 1915–
Quarterly;   cumulative   index   for   Volumes   1–20;
21–50   22.5 cm

ARRANGEMENT: The relevant section is entitled Periodical
Literature and it appears after the articles, book reviews and
notes and comments section. In the issue examined the
section covered some 13 pages. Relevant articles from a
selection of periodicals are taken and arranged in subject
sections, namely: General and Miscellaneous; Ancient;
Medieval: Reformation   and   Counter-Reformation;
Seventeenth and Eighteenth Centuries; Nineteenth and
Twentieth Centuries; United States and Canadian; and
Latin American. Within each section articles are entered
under title. Full bibliographical details are provided but
there are no annotations.

COVERAGE: The subjects covered by the articles listed relate
to aspects of Catholic History, not specifically American,
although one section is devoted to the U.S.A. and Canada.
The some 200 entries included are selected from a wide
range of periodicals, American and European, and articles
from many general and historical periodicals have been
included as well as those from the more specialized
theological and ecclesiastical history journals.

COMMENT: In the issue examined, most of the entries relate
to articles that had been published within the previous
twelve months. The only aid for using the section is the
subject arrangement. As already noted, entry within the
subject arrangement is by title (not in alphabetical order)
and there are no author entries, the result being that each
section has to be read throughout before relevant
information can be extracted. However, for those interested
in the subjects covered, the section provides a useful resumé
of articles currently being published.

Published by the Catholic University of America Press, 620 Michigan Avenue, N.E., Washington D.C. 20064, U.S.A. ISSN 0008-8080

69 The Catholic Periodical and Literature Index (CPLI)

Vol. 14–   ; 1967/8–

Continues *The Catholic Periodical Index*, a cumulative author and subject index to a selected list of Roman Catholic periodicals (Volumes 1–13, 1930/1933–1965/6). Incorporates *The Guide to Catholic Literature* (Volumes 1–8; 1888/1940–1964/7).

Six a year; twelve issues to a volume, biennial cumulations   28 cm

ARRANGEMENT: *CPLI* is an author and subject index to a selected list of Roman Catholic periodicals, and an annotated author-title-subject bibliography of adult books by Catholics, with a selection of Catholic interest books by other authors. Author, title and subject entries are arranged in one alphabetical sequence. Each bi-monthly issue contains an average of 56 pages.

COVERAGE: *CPLI* describes itself as providing 'a broad Christian approach to currently significant subjects'. It would therefore be wrong to assume that it is concerned only with matters ecclesiastical or theological. It should be seen rather as an index to Roman Catholic current awareness. As described above, books are covered, but the extent of this varies considerably from issue to issue. In the last ten issues examined the lowest number of books noticed, as indicated on the title page, was 29 and the highest was 157. Book reviews are covered, and form a significant subject division in the main sequence. Dissertations and reports are not covered. In the most recent issue examined the periodical data base contained 135 titles, of which about half are American – including some distinctly popular titles – and over four-fifths are English language.

COMMENT: Currency is excellent: the average gap is only

two to three months. The guide presents no insurmountable problems, and will commend itself particularly to Anglo-American users who are familiar with the dictionary catalogue and the Library of Congress subject headings. Although it is thoroughly professionally organized the utility of the *CPLI* is considerably reduced by the curious mixture of titles scanned.

Published by the Catholic Library Association, 461 West Lancaster Avenue, Haverford, Pennsylvania 19041, U.S.A. ISSN 0008-8285

Christian Periodical Index (ChrPI)

(A selected list.) An index to subjects, authors and book reviews
Vol. 1–   ; 1956–
Semi-annual; though was quarterly with annual cumulation, plus cumulations every five years (latest for 1971–1975)   15 cm

ARRANGEMENT: This Periodical Index has much declined during the last few years. It was at one time divided into two sections, c. 50 pages entitled Christian Periodical Index and another 20 pages per issue entitled An Index to Book Reviews. Before these sections there were published lists of the periodicals covered, the indexers' names, the abbreviations used, a sample entry and a statement of policy. The section called the Periodical Index listed subjects and authors in one alphabetical sequence and provided bibliographical details of the periodical article. There were, and are, no annotations. The second section was an alphabetical listing of authors, giving the title of the book in question, details of the periodical carrying a review of it, and the names of the reviewers. The *ChrPI* used to be a handsome volume: it is now duplicated onto A4 paper, and then photographically reduced to half-size.

COVERAGE: The policy statement mentioned above outlined the basis for selection. The emphasis was, and is, towards evangelical Christian literature and 'periodicals are chosen for their value to students training for various Christian ministries as well as to librarians and other educators interested in the field'. Some 50 periodicals now appear to be included, some of them learned, almost all American, and most with a specifically evangelical bias (including *Moody Monthly!*) though some more general ones are scanned.

COMMENT: At its best the *ChrPI* was clear, well-presented, easy to use and very up to date. Subject headings were comprehensive, and there were a considerable number of cross-references. Standards have not been maintained, and, even when the *ChrPI* was at its best, the more learned journals included in it were easily to be found in other abstracting and indexing services. It was, and may indeed still be, of value to libraries with a strongly evangelical bias, which might be interested in some of the more peripheral journals which it covers.

Published by Christian Librarians' Fellowship Inc., 910 Union Road, West Seneca, New York 14224, U.S.A.
ISSN 0069-3871

71 Cistercian Studies (CistS)
Vol. 1– ; 1966–
Quarterly   23.5 cm

ARRANGEMENT: Most issues contain a Bulletin of Monastic Spirituality at the back, while the main part of the journal is devoted to the Cistercian Order, or to spiritual life in a monastic context. Up to ten articles appear in each issue, most of them of a fairly high scholarly standard. The Bulletin is largely a series of reviews of books, some reviews being two to three pages in length. In some issues the Bulletin is devoted to a particular topic.

COVERAGE: The scope of the Bulletin is not limited to works on the Cistercians but takes in monastic spirituality in general. It is, however, limited to books, most of them in English or French.

COMMENT: The Bulletin is quite useful, but the currency is

poor: books published in 1974 were still being reviewed five years later. It should be remembered that much supplementary information can be found in *Collectanea Cisterciensia* (No. 73), a sister publication, and in *Citeaux* (No. 72).

Published by Collectanea Cisterciensia, Abbaye de Notre Dame de Paix, Chimay, Belgium
ISSN 0578-3216

Citeaux
Commentarii Cistercienses
Vol. 1– ; 1950–
Quarterly   23 cm

ARRANGEMENT: Each issue contains three or four very scholarly articles on the Cistercian Order in French, English or some other Western European language. In most issues these are followed by a Conspectus Bibliographicus given over to some broad subject, and sub-divided as necessary by place and person.

COVERAGE: The content of the bibliographies cover the Cistercian Order, and related monastic topics. No list of journals scanned has been published, though they appear to be mainly from Western Europe and the U.S.A. Fairly long abstracts are given of each item, generally in the language of the original article.

COMMENT: The currency is poor. The 1977 volume, the last to contain the Conspectus Bibliographicus, has entries dating from as far back as 1972. Many of the journals scanned, however, are uncommon, and the bibliography performs a useful function in searching them out. *Citeaux* should be used in conjunction with *Cistercian Studies* (No. 71) and *Collectanea Cisterciensia* (No. 73).

Published by Abbaye Cistercienne, CCP 000-0145276-67, B-3581 Achel, Belgium
ISSN 0009-7497

73 Collectanea Cisterciensia (CCist)

Revue de spiritualité monastique
Vol. 1– ; 1934–
Quarterly   23.5 cm

ARRANGEMENT: Each issue contains from five to ten articles on the Cistercian Order and related topics, all of which are in French. Most issues contain a Chronique Monastique giving news and information, and details of recent conferences. In most, though not in all, issues, this in turn is followed by the Bulletin de Spiritualité Monastique arranged in five sections: general studies, up to the sixth century, from the sixth to the eleventh, from the twelfth to the sixteenth and from the sixteenth century to the present day. These sections appear annually, the General Studies coming out in the first issue of each volume, and 'from the sixteenth century to the present day' in the final part. The intermediate sections do not appear on quite such a regular basis. Within the sections classification of the entries is usually by person or place. A name index is published annually.

COVERAGE: Anything to do with the Cistercians, and related monastic topics can be found in the Bulletin, and both books and articles are included. Most books appear to be in French, but English-language journals (and some American theses) are entered, with appropriate references. Each issue contains some 40 items, and most are given a page of review/abstract, articles being treated as thoroughly as books, if their importance merits it.

COMMENT: Coverage is better in the *CCist* than in *Cistercian Studies* (No. 71), especially for French and Italian material, though *Cistercian Studies* has the edge for English-language material. It is easy to use, and currency is very good, particularly for journals.

Published by Collectanea Cisterciensia, Abbaye de Notre Dame de Paix, Chimay, Belgium

Comprehensive Dissertation Index
1861–1972 (37 vols.), 1973–1977 (19 vols.)
A periodic cumulative work, but annual volumes are available from 1973

ARRANGEMENT: These two compilations are arranged in subject volumes and within each volume or set of volumes, the listing is alphabetically by keyword. Volume 32 of the larger, cumulation and Volume 16 of the smaller set cover Religion. There are multi-volume author indexes to both cumulations. Full citations appear in both the author and subject listings; these include complete title, author's full name (if known), date, university, pagination, reference to *Dissertation Abstracts International* (No. 78) or other published listing, and University Microfilms publication number for dissertations which are available from that agency.

COVERAGE: *Comprehensive Dissertation Index* attempts to list all dissertations accepted at universities of the United States during the period indicated. Many Canadian and some other foreign universities are included. It supersedes the many other lists of American doctoral dissertations and includes some dissertations not previously listed. The 1973–1977 cumulation indexes some 178,000 doctoral dissertations.

COMMENT: The lack of lower-case type makes for hard going, but as the fullest listing available over such a wide time scale, it is an indispensable resource for a thorough search of thesis material. The indexing is better than that in *American Doctoral Dissertations* (No. 10), though that will need to be consulted for the latest dissertations; and *Dissertation Abstracts International* (No. 78) has full abstracts indicating the contents of most dissertations, but lacks the convenient cumulated subject approach of *Comprehensive Dissertation Index*.

Published by University Microfilms International, P.O. Box 1764, Ann Arbor, Michigan 48106, U.S.A. *and* 18 Bedford Row, London WC1R 4EJ, U.K.

75 Current Bibliography on African Affairs

Vol. 1– ; 1967–

Quarterly; no cumulations   22 cm

ARRANGEMENT: The *Current Bibliography on African Affairs* is arranged in three main sections: a features section which has topical and bibliographic articles; a book review section; and a bibliographical section. The bibliographical section is arranged, firstly, by General Subject, of which Religion is one of the subjects, and secondly, by Regional Studies. The latter is sub-arranged by region, and then by individual country. There is an author index to the bibliographical section. Each entry in the bibliographical section has full details of author, title and bibliographical data, while some entries are given a brief abstract. Consecutive numbering of the entries facilitates reference from the author index.

COVERAGE: Coverage is said to be 'comprehensive on a multi-media basis' and covers books, reports, newspapers and journals. There is no listing of what is included or consulted. Most aspects of African life and history are included, and coverage is wide.

COMMENT: Indexing is prompt but there are no cumulations. The value of this bibliography to students of religion is hard to assess. Only 21 entries appeared in the Religion category in Volume 4.

Published for the African Bibliographic Center by the Baywood Publishing Company, Inc., 120 Marine St., P.O. Box 609, Farmingdale, New York 11735, U.S.A.
ISSN 0011-3255

76 Current Index To Journals in Education (CIJE)

Vol. 1– ; 1967–

Monthly; semi-annual cumulations   27 cm

ARRANGEMENT: The Main Entry Section lists some 10,000 entries each semi-annual cumulation, and covers over 500 pages. Each entry gives: full bibliographical details (title, author, journal title and issue details); a list of up to five subject descriptors (which are the headings used in the subject index); and, in most cases, a brief summary of the contents of the article.

The Subject Index is arranged alphabetically by subject headings (of which a full list is available in the separately published *Thesaurus of ERIC Descriptors*). Reference to the Main Entry Section is by means of a running number. The entries in the Subject Index give the full bibliographic details, but not the brief abstract. Each entry can appear under a number of subject headings. Examples of headings with the number of entries covered in the latest semi-annual volume consulted are: Christianity (3 items): Church Programs (2); Church Related Colleges (4); Church Role (2); Church Worker (1); Judaism (1); Religion (11); Religion. Cultural Groups (5); Religious Differences (2); Religious Education (15); Religious Factors (8); Religious Freedom (1); Religious Organization (1).

The Author Index is much briefer, giving only author, title and reference number to the Main Entry Section.

The Journal Content Index lists all the articles indexed arranged in order of the journals and the particular issues. A list of the journals indexed is included in the prefatory matter (Source Journal Index).

COVERAGE: *CIJE* covers more than 700 publications including both core and peripheral journals in education. The scope is international but English-language. There is a North American emphasis.

COMMENT: Monthly issues are received promptly and cover journals for the preceding months, but the semi-annual volumes, which cover the previous half-year are delayed for about another half-year. All entries are preserved on magnetic tape and are merged with the ERIC computer file and are available for on-line searching. A reprint service is available from University Microfilms International for many of the journals indexed in *CIJE*. Despite the publication delay, the comprehensiveness of *CIJE* for English-language material, the good subject indexing, and the clear presentation, make this an essential resource for tracing journal articles on religious education and its administration. Related titles are *British Education Index* (No. 51) and *Education Index* (No. 81).

Compiled by the sixteen Clearinghouses or cooperating centres of ERIC (Educational Resources Information Center) and by Macmillan Information.
Published by Macmillan Information, a division of Macmillan Publishing Co. Inc., 866 Third Avenue, New York, New York 10022, U.S.A.
ISSN 0011-3565

77 Current Research
Titles of theses and dissertations in the fields of theology and religious studies
Vol. 1–   ; 1974–
Irregular; each issue supersedes earlier issues   29 cm

ARRANGEMENT: The 1978 issue has 81 pages, of which 73 form the main subject sequence of entries for dissertations in progress. This is preceded by pages giving the list of subjects and a list of the university and college faculties and departments which have supplied the information. Each entry has a reference number, followed by author's surname and initials, then the proposed title of the dissertation, then the place, institution, faculty or department in which the work is supervised, and the degree (D.Phil., Ph.D., D.D., M.A., M.Litt., S.T.L., etc.). Within each subject heading, the entries are arranged alphabetically by author. There is no author index, though previous issues have had one.

COVERAGE: This includes all subjects connected with religion on which research is carried out within the British Isles: all ancient and modern religions; and within Christianity – Church history, Bible, theology, liturgy, spirituality, missions, philosophy of religion, semantics, ethics, and the religious aspects of psychology, sociology, education, and the arts. Entries are limited to dissertations for higher degrees reported as in progress in universities, polytechnics and colleges in Great Britain and Ireland. The 1978 issue has 1263 entries. A few appear under more than one subject heading. It would be rare for a British thesis not to be written in English.

COMMENT: There have been four duplicated-typescript issues of *Current Research*, in 1974, 1975, 1976 and 1978. Each has included many more titles than its predecessor, reflecting greater cooperation from the reporting institutions. No other source has provided information, on this scale, of work in progress in these fields.

The Institute of Religion and Theology has not yet decided whether to print a 1980 issue, but the data has been collected and stored in computer files at Sunderland Polytechnic. From January 1979 the Division of Religion and Philosophy, Sunderland Polytechnic, Chester Road, Sunderland SR1 3SD, U.K. has provided a current information service for postal inquiries on research in progress, using their computer data base. Information can be retrieved under: (1) Author's Name; (2) Thesis Title; (3) Key-word or Phrase of Title; (4) Two Key-words or Phrases; (5) Name of Institution; (6) Name of Faculty, Department, etc. Users are invoiced for each inquiry, which should be directed to the chairman of the Division of Religion & Philosophy, the Rev. James Green. (This is not an on-line service.)

Published by the Institute of Religion and Theology of Great Britain and Ireland, and obtainable from Dr. Joan Hazelden Walker (Publications & Research Secretary), Swinton Dene, Duns, Berwickshire, Scotland, U.K.

8 Dissertation Abstracts International (DAI)

Abstracts of dissertations available on microfilm or as xerographic reproductions
Vol. 30, No. 1–   ; 1969–
Previously: *Microfilm Abstracts* (1938–1951) and *Dissertation Abstracts*, (1952–1969).
Monthly; annual cumulated author index   28 cm

ARRANGEMENT: *DAI* is in three sections: Section A. The Humanities and Social Sciences; Sections B. The Sciences and Engineering; and Section C. European Abstracts. Sections B and C are not considered here.

Each monthly issue is arranged as follows: Introductory matter, including a list of cooperating institutions, details about purchasing dissertations, and a table of contents; main abstracts section; Keyword Title Index; Author Index. Part II of Issue 12 is a separately published Cumulated Author Index to issues 1–12 for the year for both Sections A and B. There are some 8000 pages of abstracts per year with two to three abstracts a page, and up to 150 pages of Keyword Title Index per monthly issue. The last twelve issues consulted revealed 333 abstracts on Philosophy and 314 on Religion and Theology.

DAI is arranged by broad, general subject categories:

IA Communication and the Arts
IIA Education
IIIA Language, Literature and Linguistics
IVA Philosophy, Religion and Theology
   Philosophy
   Religion
      General
      Clergy
      History
      Music
      Philosophy
   Theology
VA Social Sciences

COVERAGE: Coverage is exclusively 'abstracts of doctoral dissertations submitted to University Microfilms International by more than 400 cooperating institutions in the United States and Canada. Some institutions do not send all of their doctoral dissertations. Also, the various institutions began to contribute ... at different times.' (Preface). A few non-North American universities also contribute, for example, from Egypt, Australia, South Africa and Belgium (the Catholic University of Louvain). All but a very few of the abstracts are in English. Most abstracts seem to be within a year of the date of the dissertation. The delay for printing and delivery is minimal.

COMMENT: *DAI* is a voluminous publication whose size and lack of an up-to-date cumulative subject (or keyword) index make subject searching difficult. For Volumes 1–29 (1938–1969) a cumulative keyword index is provided in the eleven-volume *Dissertation Abstracts International Retrospective Index*, in which Philosophy and Religion are part of Volume V: Social Sciences. From 1970 though, the subject approach has to be by looking in the classified section and the Keyword Title Index of each monthly issue. (A more up-to-date and more comprehensive cumulation is provided by *Comprehensive Dissertation Index*, 1861–1972 (No. 74). The drawback to using this is the rather broad subject categories used and the fact that you will have to then refer 'o *DAI* for an abstract. All *DAI* entries are covered though).

Although the coverage of *DAI* is not as comprehensive as that of *American Doctoral Dissertations* (No. 10), it is still a very large listing of this important type of literature, and the abstracts are full and informative. A further advantage of *DAI* is that all dissertations listed are available for purchase or for loan through the British Library Lending Division. The publishers issue occasional lists of dissertations on various subjects and regions selected from *DAI*. Lists for Religion and Theology, and Philosophy were issued in 1978.

Published by University Microfilms International, P.O. Box 1764, Ann Arbor, Michigan 48106, U.S.A. *and* 18 Bedford Row, London WC1R 4EJ, U.K.
ISSN 0419-4209

9 Documentation Cistercienne
Irregular. Size varies

ARRANGEMENT: This is a series of books, rather than a periodical. The latest volume to have appeared at the time of writing was number 23, although the fourth fascicule of Volume 16, the *Dictionnaire des Auteurs Cisterciennes*, was published at about the same time. Each volume in the series contains a certain amount of bibliographical information, but for the purposes of this *Guide* the most useful volume is undoubtedly the regular *Bibliographie Annuelle*. This has details of books and articles about the Cistercian Order arranged under very broad headings, most of them being geographical or personal names, sub-divided where necessary by additions such as Spiritualité, Études, and so on. Most entries concerning books have been picked up from other journals, and the citations include references to reviews. In addition to the *Dictionnaire* and the *Bibliographie* already mentioned, the series includes a *Bibliographie Générale de l'Ordre Cistercienne* which, when complete, will have over 500,000 entries.

COVERAGE: Over the whole range of publications in this scholarly and valuable series the coverage of the Cistercian Order, its history and its spirituality, as well as monastic spirituality in general, is very good indeed, though the information appearing in the *Bibliographie* is necessarily somewhat dated by the time it appears in print.

COMMENT: Bibliographical detail in the *Bibliographie* is somewhat scanty; there is no author index as such, and searching through by, say, country, rather than by specific foundation in a country is not possible.

Published by Éditions Documentation Cistercienne, Abbaye de Notre Dame de St. Remy, Rochefort, France

80 The Ecumenical Review (ER)
The quarterly of the World Council of Churches
Vol. 1– ; 1948/1949–
Quarterly; annual index   24 cm

ARRANGEMENT: Each issue includes: articles, ecumenical chronicle, ecumenical diary, book reviews, books received, table of contents of significant ecumenical journals. The book review section (approximately eight pages) is in no systematic order, but the separate annual indexes in each volume list both the book authors and reviewers.

COVERAGE: Subjects include: world-wide inter-church relationships, concern of World Council of Churches in international political economic and social questions, e.g. science & technology. Extent: covers books and periodical articles. Each volume reviews approximately 40 books and lists the contents of approximately 100 issues of journals in English, French and German.

COMMENT: Entries are included within twelve months of publication. This is not of use as a systematic retrieval tool, but valuable to the ecumenical browser seeking critical opinions and current awareness.

Published by the World Council of Churches, 150 Route de Ferney, 1211 Geneva 20, Switzerland
ISSN 0013-0796

31   Education Index

Vol. 1–   ; 1929–
Monthly (except July and August); quarterly and annual cumulations. (The annual cumulations are sub-titled: 'A cumulative author subject [sic] index to a selected list of educational periodicals, proceedings, and yearbooks'. The volume numbering of the monthly issues differs from that of the annual volumes.)   26 cm

ARRANGEMENT: *Education Index* is an alphabetically arranged list of subject headings with brief bibliographical details of journal articles under the relevant subject heading. The headings and sub-headings identify subjects quite closely and there are numerous *see* and *see also* references. Under the subject headings, the details of the articles are quite concise but give the title and author of the article, the journal title, issue details and pagination. Introductory matter includes Explanatory Notes, Abbreviations of Publications Indexed, and full details of the Publications Indexed. Authors are listed in the main alphabetical sequence.

COVERAGE: Some 330 periodical titles in the field of education and in the English language are indexed.

Although primarily a periodical index, yearbooks and monographs are included. *Religious Education* and *Lutheran Education* are two specifically religious journals indexed, and under the main headings Religion and Religious there were 78 sub-headings, numerous references to other headings, and 95 articles in the 1977/78 annual volume. Education is interpreted loosely and includes libraries, publishing and denominational schools.

COMMENT: This longstanding index does seem to pick up a fair number of entries relating to religious education. Its presentation falls short of that of *Current Index to Journals in Education* (No. 76), but the alternative subject vocabulary and its more frequent occurrence in libraries justify its use for those interested in religious education and allied fields. Publishing and indexing delays are minimal.

Published by the H. W. Wilson Co., 950 University Avenue, Bronx, New York 10452, U.S.A.
ISSN 0013-1385

82 Elenchus Bibliographicus Biblicus (EBB)

Vol. 49 [Vol. 1]–   ; 1968–
EBB is the former bibliographical section of the quarterly journal *Biblica*. This constituted the final part of each issue, and was paginated separately from the rest of this journal in an asterisked sequence. Now published independently, *EBB* maintains the volume numbering sequence of *Biblica*. Annual; no cumulations

ARRANGEMENT: *EBB* invariably consists of: abbreviations, main bibliography, indexes. The last four annual volumes have contained 900-plus pages, the abbreviations and indexes taking up some twenty percent of the whole. The bibliography is arranged in 22 sections, each of which is appropriately sub-divided. The first section is given over to bibliographies; the second covers introductions to the Scriptures in general – handbooks, guides, authority, revelation and inspiration in Scripture, Canon, textual criticism, hermeneutics. The third section deals with texts and versions, and the fourth concerns itself with Apocrypha, Qumran and the Pseudepigrapha. Sections 5–8 cover the Old Testament, and Sections 9–14 the New, Section 11 being devoted to the life of Christ. Section 15 is devoted to Biblical theology. The remaining sections deal with auxiliary sciences; Biblical philology, Biblical history, Biblical archaeology and Biblical geography, as well as Post-Tannaitic Judaism, the history of Biblical sciences, and the Bible for practical use.

COVERAGE: Books and periodicals are covered in all major European languages. The last four issues have each contained in excess of 10,000 entries, and despite its Roman Catholic origins, no denominational bias is evident.

COMMENT: In general there is a three-year delay in publication. Thus the volume for 1975 appeared in 1978, and it still contained material from 1974, and much, indeed, from earlier years. Though the coverage may be thorough, it is slow. *EBB* is well indexed, and contains a full list of contents. Once the Latin headings have been assimilated it is easy to use. As was remarked above, its coverage of Biblical studies is thorough, if not unrivalled, but given the long delay in an article's finding its way into the *EBB* journals such as *New* and *Old Testament Abstracts* (Nos. 120 and 123 respectively) may well be preferred.

EBB was suspended in 1976, but resumed publication in January 1980 with the first part of a two-volume coverage for the years 1977/1978.

Published by Biblical Institute Press, Piazza della Pilotta 35, 00187 Roma, Italy

83 Ephemerides Theologicae Lovanienses (EThL)
Vol. 1– ; 1924–
Quarterly   25.5 cm

ARRANGEMENT: The *EThL* is a learned journal comprising, in addition to the articles and book reviews, a chronicle of events, publications and appointments in the world of theological scholarship. The journal section consists of some

400 pages annually, and is currently somewhat shorter than the Elenchus Bibliographicus which is paginated separately and is published in mid-year as one (or a double) fascicule of the periodical. The Elenchus is arranged under eleven very general headings which roughly correspond to the traditional divisions of a theology course in a Roman Catholic seminary. There is an index of authors.

COVERAGE: The main divisions of the Elenchus are Generalia (which includes bibliography and the history of theology); the history of religion (though not Church history); Scripture; theology (including mystical and moral theology) and Canon Law. There is also a section entitled 'Quaestiones disputatae' which takes in liturgy, catechetics and ecumenical theology. This brief outline gives only the barest indication of the range of the *EThL*. Each of the eleven major sections is broken down into half-a-dozen or more constituent parts, and several of these are further sub-divided. In the last issue of the *EThL*, for example, there were about a dozen pages on Judaism under the general heading of Old Testament Scripture, and these pages were divided into seven more sections to include sections on Qumran and rabbinic studies. Under Canon Law, to give another example, were included sections on the discipline of non-Catholic, and the Canon Law of Eastern, Churches. Some 500 periodicals are surveyed annually, and books are included in the one sequence. Festschriften and other similar books are analysed. There is a fairly obvious, though readily explicable Western European/North American bias in the choice of periodicals and books.

COMMENT: Apart from the use of Latin in the headings, which in practice should occasion a scholar little difficulty, and the rather old-fashioned structure used to organize the information contained in the Elenchus, this is one of the very best indexes to current publications in theology and related disciplines. It is well laid out, and even if only the barest bibliographical information is given, it is sufficient to identify the citation without difficulty, and the Elenchus thoughtfully provides not just a list of the journals cited, but the addresses of their publishers as well. At first sight the absence of a subject index might be a drawback, but the summary of the headings is so full that an index is scarcely necessary. Currency for journal citations is usually good, entries appearing in the list about a year after their publication, which is as soon as may be expected in an annual publication. Books frequently take rather longer, at least one year longer. If one were to purchase only one bibliography for the whole range of theological and scriptural topics, then the * EThL* is highly to be recommended above most other general bibliographies available in the field of religious studies. The whole publication is excellent value for the price charged.

Published by Ephemerides Theologicae Lovanienses, Bibliothèque de l'Université, Ladeuzeplein, B-3000 Louvain, Belgium
ISSN 0013-9513

4   **Estudios Biblicos (EstB)**
Vol. 1 (2nd series) –   ; 1941–
Quarterly; annual indexes   24 cm

ARRANGEMENT: Each issue comprises scholarly articles in Spanish, and alternate issues have a further section entitled Bibliografia. Each volume totals approximately 275 papers. The Bibliografia (about 16 pages) is divided into: (1) Book review section, which is not arranged systematically, but has an annual index of authors reviewed; (2) Revista de Revistas, selected contents of periodicals. 81 issues of periodicals were noticed in Volume 35 (1976).

COVERAGE: Subjects covered are the Bible with related studies, e.g. inter-testamental books, archaeology of Middle East. Extent: books (only); and Roman Catholic – 'Con licencia eclesiastica'. About 30 reviews per year. Works in English, French, German, Spanish, Italian.

COMMENT: The majority of books are reviewed within twelve months of publication, but some not till three years later. But publication was temporarily suspended in September 1980 after the distribution of Volume 37, Parts

3/4 (July/December 1978). Both books and periodicals are a very small selection from the field. The Bibliografía is mainly of value for the Spanish Catholic viewpoint.

Published for the Instituto Francisco Suárez of the Consejo Superior de Investigaciones Científicas, by Librería Científica Medinaceli, Duque de Medinaceli 4, Madrid 14, Spain
ISSN 0014-1437

85   **European Bibliography of Soviet, East European and Slavic Studies**
Vol. 1–   ; 1975–
Incorporates *Travaux et publications parus en français en … sur la Russie et l'URSS*, 1963–1974, and *Soviet, East European and Slavonic Studies in Britain*, 1971–1974.
Annual   20 cm

ARRANGEMENT: This specialized bibliography is classified by region, each of which is sub-divided by subject. One of the sub-divisions is Religion, which is given the section number 11.5 for each of the regions. A general section covering the whole area precedes the individual regions. Introductory matter is given in English, French and German.

COVERAGE: Coverage is the U.S.S.R. and the eight communist countries of East Europe (viz. Albania, Bulgaria, Czechoslovakia, G.D.R., Hungary, Poland, Rumania and Yugoslavia). Books, articles from journals and symposia, scholarly reviews and articles of lasting value from the daily Press are included. No listing is given of the items consulted, though the field seems very wide. Numerous languages are covered. The 1975 issue listed 218 entries under the Religion headings. Material is input .from British, French and German centres.

COMMENT: The 1975 volume covered material of that year and was published in 1977. Future continuation seems uncertain, but this is a valuable and important bibliography with a substantial coverage of religion.

Published for the International Committee for Soviet and East European Studies, by the Centre for Russian and East European Studies, University of Birmingham, P.O. Box 363, Birmingham, B15 2TT, U.K.
ISSN 0140-492X

6 Guide to Indian Periodical Literature
Vol. 1–   ; 1964–
Quarterly; annual cumulations   24 cm

ARRANGEMENT: The bibliography is arranged on the dictionary principle, with author and subjects in one sequence. The annual volume contains a helpful list of addresses of the periodicals scanned, as well as the abbreviations used for them.

COVERAGE: The scope of the *Guide* is the whole range of the social sciences and the humanities, and entries of interest specifically to students of religion are not very numerous, but they are drawn from 350 Indian periodicals, the contents of many of which would be likely to go unnoticed in the West were it not for the *Guide*. The *Guide* does not include books, as may be gathered from the title, but it lists book reviews, and gives full bibliographical information about the volume to which the reviews refer.

COMMENT: An issue of the *Guide* appears approximately six months after the period to which it refers, and even then is likely to contain citations of an even earlier date. Nevertheless, the currency is fairly good. There are usually very few entries under the heading Religion, but many more can readily be discovered by looking up associated headings such as Christianity, Sikhism and so on, or by following the *see* references. It is invaluable in guiding the researcher to what would be, in Western European or American eyes, rather out-of-the-way publications, and students of Indian religions, or of religion in India should have it drawn to their attention. It is comparatively cheap for so large an enterprise – an annual volume runs to c. 750 pages.

Published by Indian Documentation Service, Gurgaon, Haryana 122 00 1, India
ISSN 0017-5285

87 Guide to Religious Periodical Literature

Vol. 1– ; 1975–
Six times a year   21 cm

ARRANGEMENT: Originally this service provided informative abstracts from a number of theological journals, arranged by journal title and then by the order in which the articles appeared in each journal. From Volume 4 No. 2, however, this was supplemented by publishing the contents list of a larger number of theological periodicals, arranged alphabetically by periodical title.

COVERAGE: All aspects of religion are embraced, including some very useful non-Christian material. Coverage depends entirely on the holdings of the Birmingham Central Reference Library, which at present takes some 300 journals in the field. Initially a rather random selection of journals was covered, and it was difficult to foresee which would be abstracted and which not, though this seems to have settled down to about a dozen titles.

COMMENT: With the exception of a handful of non-Christian journals, this service does not cover much that is not readily available elsewhere. Currency, however, is exceptionally good. There are no indexes, so a subject approach is impossible. It is best seen, perhaps, as a current-awareness service, and probably of most use to someone working away from a good academic library.

Published by Birmingham Public Libraries, Central Libraries, Paradise, Birmingham, West Midlands, B3 3HQ, U.K.

88 Guide to Social Science and Religion in Periodical Literature

Vol. 1– ; 1964–
Until 1968 was called *Guide to Religious Periodicals* and from

1969–70 the *Guide to Religious and Semi-Religious Periodicals.*
Quarterly; there have been annual and triennial
cumulations, though not recently   27.5 cm

ARRANGEMENT: This *Guide* has a dictionary catalogue
approach, with broad subject headings divided as necessary.
There is extensive cross-referencing.

COVERAGE: Both the social sciences and religion are covered,
but those terms are used fairly loosely to include Marxism
and humanism as well. Just over 100 journals are indexed,
many of which are not specifically religious but publish
articles from time to time with a religious interest.
Indexing, therefore, of the 100-plus periodicals is selective.

COMMENT: The *Guide* is particularly useful for picking up the
occasional article published in a journal not usually
associated with religious studies. In addition, most of the
journals indexed are not of a very high scholarly standard
and are, in consequence, ignored by the majority of
bibliographic tools. Currency is good, but the arrangement
of the entries is not. Some of the terms (e.g., Evangelism,
Urgency of) do not seem particularly helpful, and the
extensive cross-referencing only irritates when a *See also*
reference refers the reader to a place in the *Guide* with no
entries.

Published by National Periodical Library, Box 47, Flint,
Michigan 48501, U.S.A.
ISSN 0017-5307

Historical Abstracts
Bibliography of the world's periodical literature
Vol. 1– ; 1953–
To 1964, covers the world's periodical literature on history
from 1775 to 1945. After 1964, the United States and Canada
are excluded and covered in *America: History and Life.*
Beginning with Volume 17 (1971), *Historical Abstracts* is
published in two parts: (A) Modern history abstracts,
1775–1914; (B) Twentieth century abstracts, 1914– .
Quarterly; Spring and Summer numbers with their own

issue indexes, and the Winter number being the cumulative annual index   28 cm

ARRANGEMENT: Parts A and B are arranged similarly. There is a classified arrangement within three sections. The first section covers history in general; the second covers topics which are too broad to go in the third and largest section, which is arranged by area and country. Religions and Churches is one of the topic headings in the second section. Abstracts and citations are numbered consecutively through the volume year and are arranged alphabetically by author within each classification section. The numbering is independent in Parts A and B. Foreign titles are translated into English.

The Subject Index consists of an average of five subject, geographic and biographic descriptors for each entry. The Author Index lists the article authors and abstract numbers. The annual cumulation, however, is not a fully integrated one, and it is necessary to look in three locations, i.e. three different page sequences per subject.

COVERAGE: Coverage is world wide except the U.S.A. and Canada. All branches of history, related social sciences and humanities, and the historical profession are encompassed. Some 2200 periodicals are selectively indexed, and abstracts of articles included in Festschriften, mélanges, transactions and proceedings are covered. The abstracts are signed and are of normal paragraph length. About 30 percent of the entries are citations rather than abstracts. There are between 70 and 90 entries in both annual cumulations under the heading Religions and Churches, while the heading Religion, -s -ous in the Part B, 1977 volume, subject index listed 81 entries.

COMMENT: The major abstracting resource for history. Publication is reasonably prompt, the abstracts are clear, and the indexing adequate. An essential work for any student of religious history.

Published by ABC-Clio Inc., P.O. Box 4397, Santa Barbara, California 93101, U.S.A., *and* Clio Press Ltd., Woodside House, Hinksey Hill, Oxford, OX1 5BE, U.K.
ISSN 0363-2725

0 Humanities Index

Vol. 1–   ; 1974–

Continues in part the *Social Sciences and Humanities Index* (1965–1974) and the *International Index* (1907–1965). A companion volume to the *Social Sciences Index* (No. 160)
Quarterly; annual cumulations   26 cm

ARRANGEMENT: The main index consists of an alphabetical arrangement of author and subject entries to periodical articles. In addition there is an author listing of citations to book reviews. The subject headings are quite specific. The 1978 annual volume had 766 pages of index entries and references and there were 200 pages of book reviews listed.

COVERAGE: 'Subject fields indexed include archaeology and classical studies, area studies, folklore, history, language and literature, literary and political criticism, performing arts, philosophy, religion and theology, and related subjects.' 261 periodicals are indexed including several generalist religious ones. Examples are *The Ecumenical Review*, *The Harvard Theological Review*, *History of Religions*, and *Interpretation: a journal of bible and theology*. A large number of entries on religious subjects are indexed; we find, for example, 6 entries and one reference under Mormons, and 15 entries and 8 references under Church Music and its sub-headings in the 1978 volume. There are a thousand entries and more perhaps for religion and theology.

COMMENT: A comparatively new indexing tool in a hitherto rather poorly covered area. *Humanities Index* can be regarded as the American counterpart to the *British Humanities Index* (No. 52) though there is some overlap in coverage. Its wide coverage of generalist journals is a useful counterpart to more specialist religious indexes and abstracting journals.

Published by the H. W. Wilson Co., 950 University Avenue, Bronx, New York 10452, U.S.A.
ISSN 0095-5981

91 Index of Articles on Jewish Studies
Vol. 1–   ; 1969–
Annual   23.5 cm

ARRANGEMENT: As with all basically Hebrew publications the *Index* opens, in Western European terms, from the back, although a title page and contents list are provided in English at what would otherwise be the front. In addition to the numbered list of citations organized under broad subject divisions, there is an index of book reviews, a subject index, and an index of authors.

COVERAGE: All aspects of Jewish studies are taken into account – bibliography, printing, the Bible, Jewish spirituality, history, liturgy, language and literature, and the State of Israel. Well over 100 Hebrew periodicals and four times that number of non-Hebrew ones are covered, many of them being neither of explicitly Jewish or religious interest. Articles appearing in 'collections' (Festschriften and similar books) are also cited. The 1978 edition of the *Index* listed over 30 Hebrew and nearly 50 non-Hebrew volumes of this sort. Most of the periodicals and books cited were published in Israel, Europe or the United States, although there is a handful from elsewhere, including the Far East. The latest edition available, that for 1978, contains 2748 entries.

COMMENT: In principle the currency is excellent. The *Index* for 1969 covered articles published in 1966, but that three-year delay has, in theory, been eliminated. The 1978 volume claims to cover material published in that same year, with additions from 1966–1977. The 'additions', however, are very much more in evidence than the citations from 1978, most of the collections, for example, having been published in 1977, and a good number of them in 1976 or even earlier. That apart, however, the *Index* provides excellent coverage of all aspects of Jewish studies even though, to make best use of it, the reader needs to be able to understand Hebrew.

Published by The Jewish National and University Library, P.O. Box 503, Jerusalem, Israel

Index to Conference Proceedings Received
Vol. 1–   ; 1966–
Monthly; ten-year cumulation for 1964–1973; annual cumulations from 1974   29 cm

ARRANGEMENT: The arrangement is alphabetically by keywords used in the titles of the conferences. The entries are much abbreviated but give the essential details of the published proceedings including the date and place of the conference. The entry also includes the shelfmark of the British Library Lending Division.

COVERAGE: The *Index to Conference Proceedings Received* is based on the material received by purchase, donation, or exchange by the Lending Division of the British Library. In most cases these are monographs, but proceedings which form part of another work, such as a journal, are included. The 1978 annual volume included some 12,000 conferences from all over the world and on a variety of subjects. Although conferences in the sciences predominate, the keywords Religion and Religious produced 40 conferences in the 1978 volume.

COMMENT: The reports of conferences are often difficult to locate, and this publication serves a useful purpose in covering this diffuse and troublesome genre. Publication is prompt and although many entries relate to earlier years, this is generally due to the tardy publication of conference proceedings. Although the proceedings of conferences on religion do not figure greatly, conference proceedings are a useful source for reports of work in progress, new developments, new thinking, and not least, for the reports of discussions which are sometimes included.

All items listed are available for loan via U.K.-registered users of the BLLD.

Published by the British Library Lending Division, Boston Spa, Wetherby, West Yorkshire LS23 7BQ, U.K.
ISSN 0305-5183

93 Index to Mormonism in Periodical Literature

Vol. 1– ; 1976–
Annual; five- and ten-year cumulations offered; microfiche

ARRANGEMENT: Each annual edition is on two microfiches, with entries arranged in dictionary fashion, authors and subjects being in the same sequence. Each entry contains author, title of article and bibliographical reference.

COVERAGE: 21 periodicals published by, or primarily about, Mormonism are scanned for articles concerning the 'Church history, scriptural commentary, biography and doctrine' of the Church of the Latter-Day Saints. Some 300 other journals are also indexed, including many non-religious titles. Full details of the 21 major periodicals are provided, in case the user of the *Index* wants to order them. Conferences are also indexed.

COMMENT: Much of the material is not at all scholarly, and information on the more learned periodicals can be obtained elsewhere. It is, however, the only bibliographical tool devoted exclusively to Mormonism, and must be a primary source for the study of that religion. The microfiche quality is good.

Published by Church of Jesus Christ of Latter-Day Saints, Historical Department, 50 East North Temple Street, Salt Lake City, Utah 84150, U.S.A.
ISSN 0148-6586

94 Index to Theses

Accepted for higher degrees by the universities of Great Britain and Ireland and the Council for National Academic Awards
Vol. 1– ; 1950/1951 –
Often referred to as the *ASLIB Index to Theses*
Annual

ARRANGEMENT: The main part of each volume is a subject sequence listing theses (dissertations) giving author, title, university, degree, year, and a reference number. There are also notes on the availability of theses at each institution, an author index, a list of subject headings and an alphabetical index to subject headings. Recent volumes extend to a little over 100 pages.

From Volume 26, Part 1 (1977) a supplement of Abstracts of Theses (U.K.) has been issued on microfiche. Abstracts are available for about 1000 of the 5000 thesis titles listed in each part. Volume 27, Part 1 (1979) also includes a subject index of 19 pages to give access at a more specific level than the index to subject headings allowed. This includes reference to topics included under headings that might not otherwise appear relevant, and removes the need for the many *see also* references previously used.

COVERAGE: All the subjects studied at higher levels in the U.K. universities, etc., are eligible for inclusion. The headings most relevant to this *Guide* are: Religion, Christian (theology, Bible, history of religion, Church history, studies of individual theologians, practical theology); Non-Christian Religions; Religious Education. About 100 entries out of 5000 fall under these headings.

Theses for higher degrees only are included, e.g. Ph.D., M.Phil., M.Sc., B.Litt. Excluded are dissertations written for a degree for which written exams are also required; and higher degrees awarded on the basis of published work. The great majority are written in English.

COMMENT: Each volume is numbered in two parts, but in most years only one part has been issued. Volume 27, Part 1 (1979) includes theses accepted from 1974–1977, the majority being dated 1977. The main difficulties have been the delays in publication and the lack (shared with most of the indexes in this *Guide*) of any cumulative index. It is hoped that the computerization of the data will improve currency and subject indexing. It is also announced (January 1980) that the data will be available on magnetic tape to allow on-line information retrieval. Inquiries should be made to: Learned Information, Besselsleigh Road, Abingdon, Oxford OX13 6EF, U.K. (Tel: Oxford 730275. Telex 837794 (INFORM G).)

Comparison with *Current Research* (No. 77) suggests either that much work on dissertations is abandoned, or that the *ASLIB Index* is only informed about a small proportion of the work done in theology.

Published by ASLIB, 3 Belgrave Square, London SW1X 8PL, U.K.
ISSN 0073-6066

95 Indice de Materias de Publicaciones Periódicas Bautistas

Vol. 1– ; 1975–
Annual   28 cm

ARRANGEMENT: Subjects and authors are in one sequence in a dictionary catalogue form, all the headings being in Spanish. Entries give only the briefest of details – author, title and bibliographical reference. The journal title is given in an abbreviated form, making it necessary to consult the list of abbreviations given at the beginning.

COVERAGE: Only 21 journals are listed, most of them published by the publisher of the *Indice*, and all of them being in Spanish. Some Baptist periodicals from Mexico, also of course in Spanish, are included.

COMMENT: Like many another highly specialized tool this gathers together information not readily available elsewhere. It is, however, very parochial in outlook. It does not include articles in other journals which might be about Spanish-speaking Baptists in Mexico or Texas. It is prepared and duplicated from a typescript copy, but the 57 pages of the 1976 volume were well laid out. The volume for 1976 appeared in 1977.

Published by Instituto Biblico Bautista Mexicana y Casa Bautista de Publicaciones, P.O. Box 4255, El Paso, Texas 79914, U.S.A.

International African Bibliography

Current books, articles and papers in African studies
Vol. 1– ; 1971–
Appeared as a supplement to the International African Institute's journal *Africa* from 1929 to 1970.
Quarterly; cumulation to Volumes 3–8 (1973–1978)
23.5 cm

ARRANGEMENT: The arrangement is basically a regional one with a general section for Africa. This latter is the only one sub-divided, and one of the divisions is Religion and Philosophy. The issues for 1979 covered 44 entries under this heading. The entries are arranged alphabetically by author within each heading. The last issue of each volume has an author index. Subject 'tracings' are given to most entries to assist subject evaluation.

COVERAGE: It covers African affairs in general. Sources are world wide, though there is a strong English-language emphasis.

COMMENT: Somewhat slighter than some of the other indexes noted but reportage is quite prompt. Some religious material may be missed through being classified with a region. Useful for those wanting specifically African material.

Published for the Library, School of Oriental and African Studies, University of London in association with the International African Institute, by Mansell Publishing, 3 Bloomsbury Place, London WC1A 2QA, U.K.
ISSN 0020-5877

International Bibliography of Political Science

Vol. 1– ; 1952–
One of the four parts of the *International Bibliography of the Social Sciences* prepared by the International Committee for Social Science Information and Documentation. The parts for Social and Cultural Anthropology and for Sociology are covered in the next two entries.
Annual; no cumulations   24 cm

ARRANGEMENT: The entries are arranged alphabetically by author within a classified arrangement. This classification is fully arrayed in the prefatory matter. The majority of the entries concerning religion are located at D.18. Religious Influences (on the Governmental process). These, and other entries that occur elsewhere in the bibliography, are all noted in the Subject Index under Religion and Politics. Reference from entries in the Subject Index, Author Index and the Classification Scheme to the main bibliography is by means of a running number.

The entries themselves give author, title, publishing and pagination details for books (or abbreviated title, date and pagination for journals). Non-English-language items are translated, and where necessary, brief annotations are given. The List of Periodicals Consulted gives the abbreviations used and the place of publication of the journals indexed.

COVERAGE: Some 1800 journals covering most countries are scanned. Books and official government publications are also included, but not unpublished works and articles published in the daily Press. The guide is bilingual (English and French). The 1976 volume detailed 4253 items of which some 38 were related to religion. The main subject areas are political science, political thought, government and public administration, the process of government, international relations and area studies. Items indexed relate to the year of the volume, or the previous year. There is a two-year delay in publication.

COMMENT: The number of entries relating to religion every year is small, but since they are conveniently grouped in the classification scheme and subject index, consultation is easy. Given the massive number of journals consulted and the wide international coverage, this *Bibliography* is an obvious resource for those interested in the relationship between politics and religion, though other sources will be needed to pick up the mainstream religious periodicals. The two- to three-year delay is a little irritating for contemporary events.

110

Published by Tavistock Publications Limited, 11 New Fetter Lane, London EC4P 4EE, U.K. *and* by the Aldine Publishing Company, 529 South Wabash Avenue, Chicago, Illinois 60605, U.S.A.
ISSN 0085-2058

International Bibliography of Social and Cultural Anthropology

Vol. 1– ; 1955–

One of the four parts of the *International Bibliography of the Social Sciences* prepared by the International Committee for Social Science Information and Documentation. The parts for Sociology and Political Science are covered in Entry Nos. 97 and 99.

Annual; no cumulations   24 cm

ARRANGEMENT: The entries in the main bibliographical section are arranged alphabetically by author within subject groups. A seven-page synopsis of the classification scheme is given in the prefatory matter. Section F covers Religion, magic and witchcraft. The main sub-sections are: F.0 General Works (27 entries); F.1 Interpretation of the universe and Mythology (59); F.2 The Great Religions (125); F.3 Primitive Religions; Rites and Beliefs (261); F.4 Magic, Witchcraft and Sorcery (37); F.5 Religious Change (104). Most of these sub-groups are further sub-divided. The numbers in brackets refer to the number of entries listed in the 1975 volume. Other entries relating to religion can be found elsewhere in the classified section. All entries can be located in the Subject Index, thus: Religion – Conversion: Africa; *and* Christianity – Magic Formulas in. Reference from the Subject Index, the Author Index and from the Classification Scheme to entries in the *Bibliography* is by a running number. A List of Periodicals Consulted is included.

Each entry contains: running number, author, title of article or book (with English translation and annotation where needed), journal title, volume number, date and pagination in the case of periodicals and place of publication, publisher, date and pagination in the case of books. Illustrations and bibliographies are noted.

COVERAGE: This *Bibliography* lists some 7000 items – books, periodical articles and some government publications – on anthropology. The journals consulted number some 845 and represent a large number of countries. Some 20–30 specialist religious journals are included, e.g. *Numen* (Leiden), *Studies in Religion* (Toronto), *Studia Islamica* (Paris), *Religion and Society* (Bangalore) and *Zeitschrift für Missions- und Religionswissenschaft* (Münster). There were some 650 entries relating to religion in the 1975 volume.

COMMENT: The majority of entries relate to the year of the volume although this is published some three years late: the 1975 volume was published in 1978 and received in September. For anyone concerned with the social history of religion and with religious phenomena, this *Bibliography* is an essential source. The full subject index and the clear subject arrangement make this work relatively easy to use.

Published by Tavistock Publications Limited, 11 New Fetter Lane, London EC4P 4EE, U.K. *and* by the Aldine Publishing Company, 529 South Wabash Avenue, Chicago, Illinois 60605, U.S.A.
ISSN 0085-2074

99   International Bibliography of Sociology
Vol. 1–   ; 1951–
One of the four parts of the *International Bibliography of the Social Sciences* series prepared by the International Committee for Social Science Information and Documentation. The parts for Anthropology and Political Science are covered in the two preceding entries.
Annual; no cumulations   24 cm

ARRANGEMENT: The entries are arranged alphabetically by author within subject groupings, of which there is a seven-page synopsis. There are headings specifically for religious topics in the Section:

13   Culture, Socialization, Social Life.
13500 Magic, Mythology. Religion.
13510 Religion. Sociology of religion. (24)
13520 Magic. Primitive religion. (11)
13530 Buddhism. Christianity. (22)
13540 Church. Religious community. Sect. (29)
13550 Clergy. Religious authority. (9)
13560 Cult. Rite. (17)
13570 Myth. Religious doctrine. (22)
13580 Religious behaviour. (20)
13590 Church and State. Religious practice. (47)

(The number to the left is the section classification number. The number to the right in brackets refers to the number of entries in the 1977 volume.) There are other headings for ethics and philosophical topics. Further entries on religious topics occur throughout the bibliography, particularly under regional divisions. All can be traced through the Subject Index where are found such entries as Clergy; Islam; Latin America – Oecumenism; Lebanon – Religious Behaviour; Priest; Protestant Church; Protestant Ethics. Reference from the Classification Scheme, Author Index and Subject Index to entries in the *Bibliography*, and from one entry to others, is by means of a running number which prefixes the entries in the *Bibliography*.

The individual entries give: running number, author, title (and English translation or annotation where necessary), periodical title with volume number, date and pagination, or, in the case of books, place of publication, publisher, year of publication and pagination. There is a 42-page List of Periodicals Consulted which gives titles, abbreviations, and place of publication.

COVERAGE: Over 1600 periodicals of world-wide origin are consulted for material on sociology. Books and official government publications are also noted. Altogether, 5681 items are listed in the 1977 edition for that year and from 1976. It is hard to estimate how many religious items are covered, but the main section 'Magic, Mythology, Religion'. lists 201 and there were perhaps another 50 elsewhere in the 1977 volume. Much, of course, depends on one's interests and definitions. A few specifically religious journals are consulted, for example *Ecumenical Review* (No. 80) and *Japan Journal of Religious Studies*, and several borderline ones such as *Islam and Modern Age*, *European Judaism* and *Istina* (No. 106).

COMMENT: The value of this *Bibliography* is for the religious items culled from the 1600 or so non-religious and multi-disciplinary journals. The broad and poorly defined subject area of Sociology is of considerable relevance to research in present-day religious practice. Obviously, this *Bibliography* must complement the more specifically religious orientated bibliographies for sociological material. See also *Sociological Abstracts* (No. 161).

Published by Tavistock Publications Limited, 11 New Fetter Lane, London EC4P 4EE, U.K. *and* by the Aldine Publishing Company, 529 South Wabash Avenue, Chicago, Illinois 60605, U.S.A.
ISSN 0085-2066

100 **International Bibliography of the History of Religions / Bibliographie Internationale de l'Histoire des Religions (IBHR)**
Vol. 1–23; 1954–1979
Annual; no cumulations   25 cm

ARRANGEMENT: As a result of gradual refinement over a number of years, *IBHR* is currently organized under ten heads: General Works; Prehistoric and Primitive Religions; Religions of Antiquity; Judaism; Christianity; Islam; Hinduism; Buddhism; Chinese Religions; Japanese Religions; Minor Religions. Each section is further divided. General Works, for example, contains encyclopaedias and dictionaries; reference works; psychology of religion; philosophy of religion; sociology of religion; phenomenology of religion; collections and miscellanies. Each volume begins with a preface and *sigla*, and concludes with an author index. Volumes have tended to increase in size latterly, but over the last ten years have contained on average rather less than 200 pages.

COVERAGE: In the course of compiling the latest volume 585 periodicals of world-wide distribution were scanned. Books, articles and book reviews are noted, and dissertations of interest are picked up via *Dissertation Abstracts International* (No. 78). Within each section entries are in alphabetical order of author, regardless of the nature of the material, and are not numbered. There are no indexes of book reviews or dissertations. No denominational bias is evident.

COMMENT: The high-sounding 'published on the recommendation of the International Council for Philosophy and Humanistic Studies and with the financial support of UNESCO by the International Association for the History of Religions', which words appear on the cover and title page, has to be put into the perspective provided by successive prefaces. These bemoan the lack of research facilities at the disposal of the *IBHR*, and the lack of formal exchange arrangements with other journals. They do much to explain the difficulties experienced by the compiler, and the failure to maintain an acceptable level of currency. The 1971 volume appeared in 1975, that for 1972 in 1978, and in 1979 the volume for 1973 was published. It was announced in June 1980 that *IBHR* would be discontinued and replaced by *Science and Religion* (No. 154A). *IBHR* is easy and pleasant to use. Its two principal disadvantages are its lack of currency, and its price which looks excessive for a thinnish volume.

Published by E. J. Brill, Postbus 9000, 2300 PA Leiden, Netherlands

International Medieval Bibliography
Vol. 1– ; 1967–
Semi-annual (annual to 1970); no cumulations   21.5 cm

ARRANGEMENT: The *Bibliography* is arranged by topic, and is sub-divided by country or area. There is an author and subject index. Each entry is provided with full bibliographical information.

COVERAGE: All aspects of medieval history (that is, from A.D. 500 to 1500) are included, and the geographical limits take in the whole of Europe, the Byzantine Empire, and Russia, but the Near East, Far East, Africa and so on are omitted except where such entries would have a direct bearing on something of interest to historians of medieval Europe. To provide this information, about 650 journals are scanned, and about 75 Festschriften, conference proceedings and other works of that sort are also analysed. Of special interest to religious studies are such headings as Hagiography, Hebrew and Jewish studies, Law (including Canon Law), the Liturgy, Religious Orders, and Theology. As noted above, each of these headings is further sub-divided by region or country.

COMMENT: This is an outstanding bibliography for the medievalist, and can be a useful one to the student of religion, particularly, perhaps, the ecclesiastical historian. It would be an obvious source to turn to in general library where the *Bibliographie* of the *Revue d'Histoire Ecclesiastique* (No. 152) was not available. Its currency is good: there is a six- to twelve-month gap between original publication of an article and its appearance in this *Bibliography*, though a few older items are occasionally noted. The only drawback of this excellent bibliographical aid is its high price.

Published by the School of History, University of Leeds, Leeds LS2 9JT, U.K.
ISSN 0074-6940

102 International Review of Mission (IRM)
Vol. 1– ; 1912–
Entitled *International Review of Missions* 1912–1969
Quarterly; annual indexes   24 cm

ARRANGEMENT: Each issue contains the following: Editorial; Articles; Documentation; Book Reviews; Bibliography. Volume 68 (1979) has 481 pages. The book reviews extend to about eight pages in each issue and there is an annual index of books reviewed. The Bibliography on World Mission and Evangelism (edited by A. F. Walls, Scottish Institute of Missionary Studies, University of Aberdeen, Scotland) is printed in a systematic arrangement: the first half by subject, the second half by geographical region or territory. There are many cross-references from subjects to territories and vice versa.

COVERAGE: The Bibliography covers Christian mission in the widest sense: relationship to other world religions; relationship to environment, society and development; forms of ministry; catechesis and pastoralia. It includes periodical articles, books, dissertations, reports. The total number of items listed, each with a running number, has varied in recent years from 800 to 1800. Some of the items have annotations, which occasionally are extensive. They are drawn from English, German, French, Dutch, and Spanish publications, and from a really international range of sources.

COMMENT: Entries are included within twelve months of publication. The Bibliography is complementary to the Survey of Current Missionary Literature in the *Bulletin of the Scottish Institute of Missionary Studies* (No. 60), under the same editor. The Survey provides reviews for a wide range of books.

Published by the Commission on World Mission and Evangelism of the World Council of Churches, 150 Route de Ferney, 1211 Geneva 20, Switzerland
ISSN 0020-8582

Internationale Bibliographie der Zeitschriften-literatur aus allen Gebieten des Wissens / International Bibliography of Periodical Literature Covering All Fields of Knowledge (IBZ)

Vol. 1–   ; 1963/4–
A continuation of the *Bibliographie der Deutschen Zeitschriftenliteratur*, 1896–1964, and the *Bibliographie der Fremdsprachigen Zeitschriftenliteratur*, 1911–1964.
Semi-annual   25 cm

ARRANGEMENT: Each semi-annual volume is arranged in four sections:

A. Periodica. A list of periodical titles consulted. Each is given a key number which is used for the index entries instead of title abbreviations.
B. Index Rerum. The major sequence of *IBZ*, covering three to four volumes, which is a classified arrangement of subject headings. The subject headings are in German but references are provided from the English terms. Each entry gives the author, title, journal key number, volume, issue and pagination.
C. Index Auctorum. An index of articles arranged by author surnames.
D. Index Systematicus. A systematic index of keywords. The keywords used in the Index Rerum are distributed among 35 main subject groupings. Number 3 is Religion, Theologie, in which some 1200 keywords are listed.

COVERAGE: *IBZ* is a subject index to world periodical literature. It covers all subjects and many languages. The running number allocated to periodical titles in the Periodica has now reached 39989 and although many titles have ceased since being covered, the number of titles covered currently is still impressive. The number of keywords for religion and theology is some 1200, and the subject heading Bibel in the main index noted some 68 items in the last half-yearly issue consulted.

COMMENT: However regarded, *IBZ* is a truly impressive work. Despite the German language bias (and cross-references from the English spellings of the subject headings help to offset this difficulty), any serious researcher should use this index. The entries are a little cryptic, but the wide coverage of German and continental European journal literature make this an essential work of reference.

Published by Felix Dietrich Verlag, Jahnstrasse 15, Postfach 1949, Osnabrück, Federal Republic of Germany
ISSN 0020-9201

4 Internationale Ökumenische Bibliographie / International Ecumenical Bibliography /Bibliographie Oecuménique Internationale / Bibliografia Ecuménica Internacional (IOB)

Vol. 1/2– ; 1962/63–
Irregular; no cumulation   25 cm

ARRANGEMENT: The main section of each volume is a classified bibliography. The subject headings and preliminary matter are repeated in all four languages of the title. The preliminaries include a detailed classified table of contents, preface, instructions for use and abbreviations for periodicals. At the end is an author index, supplementary list of periodicals, full subject index in German and shortened subject indexes in English, French and Spanish, which refer back to the German index for a full list of entries. Volume 10/11 has 587 pages.

The main entries are arranged under headings and sub-headings, and then alphabetically by author. Each entry has a running number, full bibliographical details, contents lists (for composite works), and, in many cases, notes or abstracts. These are in one of the four languages used, and signed by the abstractor.

COVERAGE: All the subjects listed are included from the point of view of Church unity or at least cooperation between different Church traditions. They are – the idea of unity; World Council of Churches; the Catholic Church, Orthodox Churches, Ancient Eastern Churches, Reformed Churches, Anglican Communion, (all with territorial subdivisions); Church history, relations with non-Christian religions (specified); theological questions: Holy Scripture, Christ, Holy Spirit, Sin, Creation, faith; sacraments, liturgy, pastoral care, religious education, evangelism, ethics. Books, dissertations and periodical articles are all included. The 1971/72 volume (No. 10/11) has 4442 entries. About 600 periodicals are indexed. Items in many European languages are included and the sources of publication are appropriately world wide.

COMMENT: Volume 10/11 (1971/72) indexes items from 1971

119

and 1972 as its title claims, though a few 1970 and 1969 items are included. But the volume was not published till 1977 (and received in U.K. in October, 1977). The Preface looked forward to the publication of a volume for 1973–1975, but, three years later, this had not yet been published. The value of *IOB* as a current bibliography is diminishing rapidly. The alternative is the Ecumenical Abstracts of the *Journal of Ecumenical Studies* (No. 110). This is not nearly so comprehensive (especially of non-American material), and is not arranged systematically by subject, but it is at least up to date. *The Ecumenical Review* (No. 80) is also helpful for a very selective current awareness.

Published jointly by a Protestant and a Catholic firm: Chr. Kaiser Verlag, Postfach 509, 8000 München 43, Federal Republic of Germany; *and* Matthias-Grünewald-Verlag, Postfach 30 80, 6500 Mainz, Federal Republic of Germany ISSN 0341-9037

105 **Internationale Zeitschriftenschau für Bibelwissenschaft und Grenzgebiete / International Review of Biblical Studies /Revue Internationale des Études Bibliques (IZBG)**
Vol. 1–   ; 1951/52–
Annual; no cumulations   24 cm

ARRANGEMENT: Abstracts or index entries comprise the whole of each volume of about 400 pages. The entries are arranged in systematic subject order under headings and sub-headings in German. A final section in each volume gives details of the sequence of subjects. Under each sub-heading the entries are neither in alphabetical or chronological sequence but have a prominent identification number. Some apparently self-explanatory titles are not annotated. Others have brief notes of contents, summaries, or extracts from the author's preface. Some, perhaps ten percent, have substantial abstracts signed by the initials of one of the contributing editors, who are listed at the beginning. The notes or abstracts are in German, English or

French. The majority of the contributors appear to be German.

There are also indexes to the periodical titles indexed, to the actual issues indexed, to the author or title of each article indexed (giving its identification number), and to the authors of bibliographical or review articles.

COVERAGE: All aspects of Bible study are covered, both Canonical and Apocryphal texts. Biblical theology, archaeology, epigraphy, linguistics, with the history and culture of Israel and its neighbours in the ancient Middle East, are included.

Periodical articles and articles in Festschriften only are analyzed. Volume 23 contains 2928 entries, Volume 24 2829 entries. About 450 periodicals from all European countries and many other parts of the world are listed. The languages of the original articles include Rumanian, Russian, Polish, Greek and Afrikaans.

COMMENT: Volume 24 (1977/78) was received in October 1978. Most of the articles indexed were published in 1976, with some from 1975, and a few from earlier years. Familiarity with German is a help in using this guide for subject retrieval and for many of the abstracts. *New Testament Abstracts* (No. 120) and *Old Testament Abstracts* (No. 123) between them cover much the same ground in English and include books, but the latter is only recent and there are 24 volumes of *IBZ* available. *Elenchus Bibliographicus Biblicus* (No. 82) has no annotation but included over 8000 entries a year till its temporary suspension after the 1976 volume.

Published by Patmos Verlag, 400 Düsseldorf 1, Postfach 6213, Federal Republic of Germany
ISSN 0074-9745

6   Istina (Ist.)

Vol. 1– ; 1954–
Quarterly   24 cm

ARRANGEMENT: *Istina* is a journal dedicated to ecumenical

studies in general, but in practice it appears to have a strong bias towards Roman Catholic–Orthodox relations. Each issue, often gathered around a single topic, contains articles and documents, followed by a section called Bibliographie, although this is no more than a handful of book reviews. At least once a year, however, and occasionally more often there is published after the Bibliographie a Chronique Oecuménique des Périodiques. This is organized under four sections: Biblical, Theological and Jewish Studies; Relations with Eastern Churches; Anglicanism and Protestantism; Ecumenism and the Study of religion. The Chronique surveys a number of periodicals and provides sometimes quite lengthy but usually very brief abstracts of articles of special interest for ecumenical studies.

COVERAGE: All aspects of ecumenism are surveyed under the general headings given above, but the section on relations with the Eastern Churches is particularly valuable, taking account, as it does, of a number of journals which are not generally available. No list of journals covered by the Chronique has been published, but it would not appear to be large, and seems to be entirely European. Articles are usually cited within a year of their first publication.

COMMENT: *Istina* makes no claim that its Chronique is in any way exhaustive, and it clearly is not. Its usefulness is further limited by there being no index. Nevertheless, it provides a service to those who would purchase the journal for other reasons, and is particularly helpful to anyone interested in keeping up to date with developments in East–West Church relations. But for general ecumenical studies a researcher would be better advised to turn to the abstracts contained in the *Journal of Ecumenical Studies*, (No. 110), despite the drawbacks involved in using this tool. These comments, however, are limited only to the Chronique, and are in no way intended to disparage *Istina* as a periodical, or as a source for documents on ecumenical affairs.

Published by Centre d'Études 'Istina', 45 Rue de la Glacière, F-75013 Paris, France
ISSN 0021-2423

Jahrbuch für Liturgik und Hymnologie (JLH)
Vol. 1– ; 1955–
Annual; no cumulations   24.5 cm

ARRANGEMENT: Each volume contains about two dozen scholarly articles, followed by a major bibliography – or rather, by two bibliographies, since liturgy and hymnology are treated separately. Each one of the two bibliographies is arranged by topic and date, and further sub-divided by country.

COVERAGE: Most aspects of liturgical studies and hymnology appear to be covered by the *JLH*, and the bibliographies contain both books and journals. Although there is no list of the latter, it would seem that only the central publications in the field are scanned, and that the interest of the *JLH* is predominantly in the German-speaking lands. There is, however, some coverage of the U.S.A., of the United Kingdom, and of other parts of Europe.

COMMENT: It must be stressed that the *JLH*'s interest is primarily scholarly, unlike, say, the *Rivista Liturgica* (No. 154) or the *Questions Liturgiques* (No. 133). Its interests, too, are pretty solidly German, and this affects the currency of the material covered. Thus there is a longer delay in listing material from, say, Hungary, than there is for material from Germany itself, which is quite up to date.

Published for the International Fellowship for Research in Hymnology, by Joannes Stauda, Heinrich Schutz Allee 33, 3500 Kassell Wilhelmshöhe, Federal Republic of Germany
ISSN 0075-2681

8 Journal for the Study of Judaism
In the Persian, Hellenistic and Roman period
Vol. 1– ; 1970–
Semi-annual   24 cm

ARRANGEMENT: Scholarly articles on classical Judaism in English, French or German, form the greater part of each issue. Each volume contains about 250 pages. Each issue also contains a Review of Books, i.e. substantial book reviews, plus a list of other publications sent to the editors, and a Review of Articles – a summary of relevant articles in the latest issues of other periodicals. The reviews are not arranged by subject or chronologically. There is no cumulation and they are not indexed.

COVERAGE: The subjects covered are: Old Testament; Apocrypha; Intertestamental Books; Early Rabbinic Judaism; Judaism in the Persian, Hellenistic and Roman Periods; and the relevant archaeology and linguistics, e.g. for Aramaic, Qumran, etc., texts. About 25 books and 30 periodical articles are reviewed in each issue. They are drawn from all European languages as well as modern Hebrew.

COMMENT: Most books and articles are received within twelve months of publication. A very scholarly approach to the literature, but designed to help the expert keep up to date, not to facilitate systematic searches for information on a specific topic.

Published by E. J. Brill, Oude Rijn, Leiden, Netherlands
ISSN 0047-2212

109 Journal of Church and State (JChS)
Vol. 1– ; 1959–
Three times a year; no cumulations   23 cm

ARRANGEMENT: Each issue of the journal contains c. 200 pages including some six articles, a book review section and a section entitled Notes on Church-State Affairs which is arranged alphabetically by country. Following these is the relevant bibliographical section, Recent Doctoral Dissertations in Church and State, which usually covers two to three pages. The arrangement is alphabetical by author, and each entry includes: the title of the dissertation, the awarding university, date and pagination. There are no annotations.

COVERAGE: The subjects covered are aspects of Church and

State. Of the 25 dissertations listed all are American and all are in the English language. The interest is mainly American although a few of the entries relate to other countries and also to the subject of Church and State in other religions than Christianity.

COMMENT: The dissertations included are for the most part dated for the year prior to the publication of the issue of the journal; the section therefore provides a brief résumé of current research in the field.

Published by J. M. Dawson Studies in Church and State of Baylor University, Box 380, Baylor University, Waco, Texas 76703, U.S.A.
ISSN 0021-969X

10 Journal of Ecumenical Studies (JES)
Vol. 1– ; 1964–
Quarterly   23 cm

ARRANGEMENT: Each issue contains scholarly articles and three out of four issues contain book reviews; young people's book reviews; ecumenical abstracts; and 'ecumenical events'. Each volume contains about 700 pages. The Book Reviews total about 70 pages in the 1977 volume. The Ecumenical Abstracts (of periodical articles) in 1977 totalled 109 pages. The Book Reviews are not in any systematic order, but the Abstracts are arranged by country of publication, then by title of the periodical. Each review and abstract is fully signed. There are no subject or cumulative indexes to the reviews or abstracts.

COVERAGE: The scope is interchurch relationships of Christian bodies at local, national and world levels, and interfaith relationships at all levels. The extent covers books and periodicals as indicated above. Each volume has approximately 400 periodical abstracts and 90 book reviews.

COMMENT: Most of the periodical articles abstracted date from the previous twelve months, and most of the books reviewed from the previous two years. Admirable for the

browsing ecumenist, but inadequately arranged for
systematic searches.

Published by 511 Humanities Building, Temple University,
Philadelphia, Pennsylvania 19122, U.S.A.
ISSN 0022-0558

111 No entry

112 Journal of Psychology and Judaism (JPJUD)
Vol. 1– ; 1976–
Quarterly; no cumulations   22.5 cm

ARRANGEMENT: Each issue of the journal contains c. 100
pages and includes some six articles. The relevant
bibliographical section follows the articles and is entitled
The Critical Review in Psychology and Judaism; this covers
around 20 pages. An introduction outlining the purposes of
the review precedes the review section which is arranged by
subject. The subject headings used vary with each issue of
the review. For example, in the first issue, headings include:
General Syntheses between Psychology and Judaism; Freud
and Jewishness; History of Psychology, Rabbinical Thought
in the Light of Modern Psychology and so on. The second
issue of the review uses only three subject divisions, namely,
Clinical, Conceptual and Historical. Within the subject
arrangement entries are arranged alphabetically by author.
Bibliographical details are provided in each entry and each
item entered is annotated, each annotation being on
average 100–200 words.

COVERAGE: The subject coverage of the Review deals with
the interaction between psychology and religion,
particularly Judaism, on a clinical as well as a philosophical
level. Psychiatry, psychology, clinical social work and
religious studies are all covered. The review does not
attempt to aim at exhaustive coverage of these subjects but
is selective. Books and periodical articles are included. In the
issues examined an average of 40 items were entered,
mainly of American origin.

COMMENT: The review includes retrospective as well as current material. It is selective and is designed to 'serve as a stimulus for further reading, research and critical analysis' as well as being a reference tool. As such, it provides a guide to publications for those interested in the subject field covered.

Published for the center for the Study of Psychology and Judaism, CN, by Human Sciences Press, 72 Fifth Avenue, New York 10011, U.S.A.
ISSN 0700-9801

13 Justice Ministries
Resources for urban mission
Vol. 1–   ; Summer 1978–
An offshoot of the *Abstract Service of the Institute on the Church in Urban–Industrial Society* (No. 2).
Quarterly; annual indexes intended; mimeographed
28 cm

ARRANGEMENT: There is one article in each issue plus a series of long abstracts (average 300 words). The latest issue has 42 pages. Entries are in broad subject groupings. All are referred to by running number. Photocopies of documents can be obtained either from original publisher or I.C.U.I.S.

COVERAGE: Subjects included are: urban mission; urban disinvestment; inner-city re-invigoration; profiles of particular (U.S.) cities; ethics of energy use; energy and employment; conservation of energy; housing associations; city centre work with 'Blacks, White ethnics and Hispanics' and poor Whites. Materials included are: reports, reprints, conference papers, periodical articles, books. *Justice Ministries* has an ecumenical stance. The latest issue seen has 36 abstracts. They all refer to items in English dealing with North American urban areas.

COMMENT: Half of the abstracts are of documents published within the previous three months, three-quarters within six months, and all within two years. The selection of documents for abstracting appears to preclude viewpoints that are sociologically or theologically conservative.

Published by the Institute on the Church in Urban–Industrial Society, 5700 South Woodlawn Avenue, Chicago, Illinois 60637, U.S.A.
ISSN 0161-6072

114 Kiryat Sefer (QS)
Vol. 1– ; 1924–
Quarterly 23.5 cm

ARRANGEMENT: This quarterly regularly consists of four sections: Current Bibliography of Israel Publications and Judaica–Hebraica Abroad; Book Reviews; Studies in Bibliography and Jewish Booklore; and From the Library's Collection. The first of these is by far the longest section, and is the one of interest here. It takes up about three-quarters of the pages of this journal, and provides a list of books on Jewish studies in the broadest sense – together with more general works on any subject published in Israel – often with annotations in Hebrew. As with all Hebrew publications, QS opens from the back, by Western European standards.

COVERAGE: Although the QS only takes in books, leaving periodicals to the *Index of Articles on Jewish Studies* (No. 91), it does list periodicals as such, if they are concerned with Judaica, though not their contents. All aspects of Jewish studies are of interest to QS – Biblical studies, philosophy, spirituality, history, language and literature, and the State of Israel. The subject divisions are fairly detailed, but there is no subject index. Well over 5000 items are cited annually, including publications in Russian, Arabic and Greek as well as Hebrew and the Western European languages.

COMMENT: The lack of a subject index is a serious drawback to the use of this periodical, and to utilise it fully the reader needs to be able to understand Hebrew. Not all entries are annotated, and for the most part the annotations that are published do little more than draw attention to the contents

of the volumes cited. For works published in Israel itself
currency is, naturally enough, quite excellent, but it is
generally good for the whole range of entries, the date
between publication and appearance in *QS* rarely being
more than a couple of years. Together with the *Index of
Articles on Jewish Studies* (No. 91), produced by the same source,
the *QS* provides full coverage of Judaica.

Published by the Jewish National and University Library,
P.O. Box 503, Jerusalem, Israel
ISSN 0023-1851

15 Lutherjahrbuch (LuB)

Organ der internationalen Lutherforschung
Vol. 1– ; 1919–
Annual   22 cm

ARRANGEMENT: Each volume (about 200 pages) contains
scholarly articles, conference reports, book reviews and a
Lutherbibliographie of 40 pages. The Lutherbibliographie
is arranged by a detailed scheme of classification, followed
by supplementary entries for the bibliography of previous
years. Full bibliographical details are given, but no
annotations.

COVERAGE: All aspects of the life and work of Martin Luther
(1483–1546) and the Reformation in Germany. To a lesser
extent: the Reformation in other countries; the Counter-
Reformation; contemporary reformers, e.g. Müntzer and
Zwingli; Lutheran doctrine and Lutheran churches in later
periods. Books, theses, periodical articles, book reviews are
included. Each volume has about 800 entries, from
European and other sources, including Japan. Titles not in
German or English have German translations added.

COMMENT: About half the entries date from the two years
prior to publication, the rest from earlier years. The
Lutherbibliographie is edited at the Karl-Marx University of
Leipzig (German Democratic Republic) with a world-wide
team of contributors. For this subject area the
Literaturbericht of the *Archiv für Reformationsgeschichte* (No. 24)

might suffice in most libraries, but the Lutherbibliographie is more detailed in its own particular focus.

Published by Vandenhoeck & Ruprecht, Theaterstrasse 13, D-3400 Göttingen, Federal Republic of Germany.

116 Medieval Archaeology
Journal of the Society for Medieval Archaeology
Vol. 1– ; 1957–
Annual   24 cm

ARRANGEMENT: It is the indexes to the articles in this journal that concern us here. These are produced in cumulated form at five-yearly intervals. The latest one covers 1972–1976. Each index has two sections: General and Topographical. The General Section covers all objects, types of sites, persons, authors of articles, of books reviewed and of reviews. The Topographical Section covers places in the British Isles. The index is detailed, with subject headings and sub-headings arranged alphabetically. An example is:

churches, chapels, cathedrals and minsters
—early Christian

Cross-references are supplied, e.g. 'friaries *see* monastic sites'. The 1972–1976 index has 52 pages.

COVERAGE: Medieval archaeology is defined as being post-Roman and covering what is popularly known as the Dark Ages. Coverage is restricted to the British Isles. Only articles in the journal *Medieval Archaeology* are covered, but these are indexed in some depth and are much concerned with early Church history. It is hard to quantify the amount of religious material in the index, but there were, for example, eight references under the heading Altars and Parts of, Saxon and Early Christian.

COMMENT: The coverage of Medieval Archaeology is obviously restricted in period, location, and to the journal's articles themselves, and will have to be complemented by other archaeological and historical sources such as the *Archaeological Bibliography for Great Britain and Ireland* (No. 18).

The usefulness of the detailed indexing and five yearly cumulations, however, make this a useful source.

Published by the Society for Medieval Archaeology, c/o University College London, Gower Street, London WC1E 6BT

7 **Middle East Journal (MEJ)**
Vol. 1– ; 1947–
Quarterly; no cumulations   23.5 cm

ARRANGEMENT: The *MEJ* publishes what might be called 'middle-brow' articles on Middle-Eastern matters, followed by a chronology of events arranged by country. These, in turn, are followed by a Political Review. The section of the *MEJ* of interest here succeeds the Political Review. Under the heading Book Reviews there is, in addition to the usual notices, a list of Recent Publications. The list makes no claim to be exhaustive, and is similar to the 'Books Received' commonly found in periodicals. It is, however, up to date and seemingly fairly thorough, though with material coming from so many different sources, and countries of the Middle East, it is not easy to judge. The list is divided up according to country and, in some cases, by subjects. One of the headings is Religion, Philosophy, Science, and of the approximately twenty titles to be found there the majority are concerned with the first two terms of the heading, rather than with the third. Arabic titles are transliterated, and translations provided. The Bibliography of Periodical Literature comes after the book review section, and again the same heading Religion, Philosophy, Science is used. Anonymous entries are listed first, the others follow in alphabetical order of author.

COVERAGE: A list of periodicals scanned is published in the autumn issue of each year. The latest one available indicates that some 300 provide the resources for the bibliography. Most of them are learned journals, but others of the 'middle-brow' variety are also included. The spread, given the area of interest of the *MEJ*, is very wide geographically.

COMMENT: The number of pages devoted to the periodical bibliography is not great – some twenty in each issue – and there is no over-all index, which makes use of the *MEJ* for bibliographical purposes somewhat difficult. The currency of the citations from journals is very good, rather better than that of the book section. Interest is not limited to Islam, though obviously that plays the largest part in the *MEJ*, but material on both Christianity and Judaism in the Middle East can also be found. The chronology of events, which is careful always to provide a source, usually a newspaper, for the information conveyed, is also of interest to the student of religious affairs. This is a journal well worth keeping in mind when studying the religions of the Middle East. Some of the information it contains on books, periodicals and events will not readily be found elsewhere.

Published by the Middle East Institute, 1761 N St., N.W., Washington D.C. 20036, U.S.A.
ISSN 0026-3141

118   Le Moyen Âge (MA)

Revue d'histoire et de philologie
Vol. 1–   ; 1880–
Quarterly   23 cm

ARRANGEMENT: Each issue contains scholarly articles, Bibliographie, Comptes Rendus, and Ouvrages Reçus. Each volume has about 600 pages. The book review sections, totalling about 120 pages, are not systematically arranged, but are included in the annual index. The bibliography is in two parts, the first being a series of literature surveys, and the second a list of periodical articles arranged by subject, entitled Travaux Relatifs à l'Histoire du Moyen Âge.

COVERAGE: The subject fields are the history, literature and ideas of Europe in the medieval period. The periodical indexes have from 150–250 entries. The book reviews and literature surveys cover mainly books in major European languages.

COMMENT: The entries in the periodical indexes are mainly for the previous twelve months. This is not an easy guide for the searcher on specific religious topics, although a large amount of material on a wide range of topics is referred to.

Published with the support of the Fondation Universitaire de Belgique and the Centre National de la Recherche Scientifique (Paris) by La Renaissance du Livre S.A., Place du Petit Sablon 12, 1000 Bruxelles, Belgium
ISSN 0027-2841

Muslim World (MW)

A journal devoted to the study of Islam and of Christian–Muslim relationship in past and present
Vol. 1– ; 1911–
Quarterly; no cumulations   22.5 cm

ARRANGEMENT: Articles, book notes and an information service precede the survey of periodical literature, which runs to four to five pages in an issue of c. 70 pages.

COVERAGE: Only articles are listed. They are drawn from a (geographically) wide-ranging selection of periodicals, most of them learned, though not all. Some of the journals are not easily found, and the MW serves a useful purpose in drawing particular attention to these. The topics included, under ten very broad subject headings, include politics and sociology as well as more religious themes such as theology, and the relationship between Islam and other religions, particularly Christianity.

COMMENT: The survey of periodicals in MW goes back to its beginnings, but the present, numbered, series, dates from April 1967 and a change of editor. It is not clear what the value of numbering the entries can be, since there is no index to them. The number of entries is fairly small, only some 60 an issue, but the currency is very good – it could almost serve as a 'current awareness' service, along with the MW's section on information from the world of Islam.

Published by Duncan Black MacDonald Centre, Hartford Seminary Foundation, Hartford, Connecticut 06105, U.S.A. ISSN 0027-4909

120 New Testament Abstracts (NTA)

Vol. 1–   ; 1956–
Three issues a year; cumulative index to Volumes 1–15 (1956–1971)   23 cm

ARRANGEMENT: Each issue is divided into two parts, periodical abstracts and book notices, and each part is further divided into five general sections: N.T. General; Gospels–Acts; Epistles–Revelation; Biblical Theology; N.T. World. Each of these five sections is then given a series of more detailed sub-headings. The third issue of each year contains in addition the indexes – main scripture texts, authors, book reviews, book notices. Over the last ten years volumes have averaged some 400 pages.

COVERAGE: Over 300 periodicals are named in the list of journals which appears at the end of each issue, and an editorial note advises that many other periodicals in religion and the humanities are regularly surveyed for articles of interest to New Testament scholars. The range is thus clearly extensive, and no denominational bias is evident. Coverage is world wide, but there is a strong American representation. Abstracts are always in English whatever the language of the original, and are numbered. The 1979 volume contained 1075 abstracts.

COMMENT: Most of the material covered made its original appearance in the previous year, and occasionally items published in the current year have been noticed. Compared with other journals, therefore, the currency of *NTA* is impressive. Access to the material is greatly facilitated by the use of bold running heads (or, more accurately since they appear at the bottom of the page, running feet). *NTA* is unrivalled and, complemented by *Old Testament Abstracts* (No. 198) is obligatory for any library which takes its Scripture collection seriously.

Published by the Executive Office of the Council on the Study of Religion, Wilfrid Laurier University, Waterloo, Ontario N2L 3C5, Canada
ISSN 0028-6877

1 Novum Testamentum (NT)
An international quarterly for New Testament and related studies
Vol. 1– ; 1956–
Quarterly; no cumulations   24 cm

ARRANGEMENT: Each volume consists, in the main, of scholarly articles and book reviews, together with the occasional editorial. From Volume 13 (1971) NT has acted as the vehicle for David M. Scholer's Bibliographia Gnostica: Supplementa, by means of which he annually up-dates his *Nag Hammadi Bibliography 1948–69* (Leiden: Brill, 1971). In the present context our interest in the NT is limited to the Bibliographia. Each supplement is divided into four sections: General Works (= Chapters 1 and 5 of the *Nag Hammadi Bibliography*); Gnostic texts, Pre-Nag Hammadi, Schools and Leaders (= Chapters 2 and 3); the New Testament and Gnosticism (= Chapter 4) and the Coptic Gnostic Library (= Chapter 6). Within each section the material is arranged on the pattern followed in the *Nag Hammadi Bibliography*, and the enumeration of entries also continues that employed in the *Bibliography*. The last entry in the *Bibliography* was No. 2425, and the first of the first Supplementum is 2426r (r = book review). The supplements normally appear in the last issue of each year, and occupy some 20 pages out of an average total for the NT of some 350 pages.

COVERAGE: Each supplement provides a classified listing of books, reviews, articles and dissertations on the subject of gnosticism which have appeared the previous year, together with older material not yet recorded, and additions and corrections to entries in the original *Nag Hammadi Bibliography*. The scope of the supplements is that of the *Bibliography*. Thus material on Hermetic literature,

135

Mandaeism, Manichaeism, Hellenistic magical literature and Jewish literature is excluded, as is material on Cerdo and Marcion, Bardesanes, the Encratites, the Odes of Solomon etc. Medieval and modern manifestations of gnosticism, along with theosophical and anthroposophical treatments of the gnostic phenomenon are also left out, and so are writings with only occasional references to gnosticism. Some 115 periodicals are scanned, as also is *Dissertation Abstracts International* (No. 78). Supplementum VIII in *NT* 21 for 1979 takes the number of entries to 4417, thus giving an average for each supplement of 146 or so citations.

COMMENT: The gap between original appearance and listing in the supplements may vary from 9 to 21 months, but the time factor may be less important in this field of study than in some others. It is possible to use the supplements without recourse to the original *Bibliography*, but to derive maximum benefit the original *Bibliography* and the supplements should be used in conjunction. As with many other specialized works, it is unrivalled in its completeness, and in the organization of its material.

Published by E. J. Brill, Postbus 9000, 2300 PA Leiden, Netherlands
ISSN 0048-1009

122 Ökumenische Rundschau (ÖR)
Vol. 1– ; 1952–
Quarterly   21cm

ARRANGEMENT: The major part of each issue is taken up with scholarly articles. Each issue also has a short Zeitschriftenschau and a section of reviews, Neue Bücher. Each volume has about 500 pages, of which about 25 cover periodical articles and about 60 cover books. The former are not in systematic order, but the book notices are arranged under subject headings, and there is a cumulated index of all books noticed in each volume. The text is all in German.

COVERAGE: Subjects covered are world-wide interchurch and interfaith relationships, the World Council of Churches, and political, social, and economic questions from an international Christian point of view. About 120 periodical articles are listed each year, some with substantial abstracts, others unannotated. The book review section covers about 80 titles a year, each review or notice being signed. Most of the books and articles are from German-language sources, but items in English, French and other European languages are noticed also.

COMMENT: Many items are listed within six months of publication, others up to two years later. Some knowledge of German is necessary to use these reviews. This guide lacks the systematic approach of the *Internationale Ökumenische Bibliographie* (No. 104), but is far more up to date. It is complementary to the *Ecumenical Review* (of the World Council of Churches (No. 80)) in its German orientation, but very much less comprehensive than the Ecumenical Abstracts in the (American) *Journal of Ecumenical Studies* (No. 110).

Published by Verlag Otto Lembeck, Leebachstrasse, 6000 Frankfurt am Main 1, Federal Republic of Germany
ISSN 0029-8654

Old Testament Abstracts (OTA)
Vol. 1– ; 1978–
Three a year; no cumulations   23 cm

ARRANGEMENT: Each issue is divided into two parts. The first contains periodical abstracts, the second has book notices. Each part is further divided. The material of the periodical abstracts is organized under ten headings: General; Archaeology, Epigraphy, Philology; History and Geography; The Pentateuch; Historical Books; The Writings; Major Prophets; Minor Prophets; Biblical Theology; Intertestamental and Apocrypha. The second part consists of eight sections: Introduction and General; Pentateuch; Historical Books; The Writings; The Prophets;

Biblical Theology; Varia; Other Books Received. The third issue of each year contains in addition the indexes of authors, of Scripture references, and of Semitic words. The first volume contained 867 abstracts in 328 pages.

COVERAGE: About 250 journals are currently abstracted, almost all of them scholarly and emanating from all quarters of the globe. There is no evidence of denominational bias. Abstracts are always in English, whatever the language of the original, and abstractors are named. Unlike, say, *Religious Index One: Periodicals* (No. 137), no attempt is made to persuade the authors of the original articles to provide their own abstracts.

COMMENT: In principle January 1977 was set as the starting date for coverage. In practice some earlier material has been reviewed. In general, the gap between publication and the appearance of an abstract or review appears to be about a year, but this time lag may well lengthen as successive issues pick up earlier material which has only just come to the notice of *OTA*. The guide is simple to use, and the only pity is that it has taken twenty-one years for *New Testament Abstracts* (No. 120) to be complemented in this fashion.

Published by The Catholic University of America, Washington, D.C. 20064, U.S.A.
ISSN 0364-8591

124 OT/ANE Permucite Index

An exhaustive interdisciplinary indexing system for Old Testament studies [and] ancient Near East studies
Vol. 1, Part 1– ; 1978–
Intended to appear three times a year, with annual cumulations of the citation, permutitle, author and research centre indexes   32 cm

ARRANGEMENT: Each part (strongly bound) has a general introduction to citation indexing, and to the use of this *Index*; a list of journals scanned, with abbreviations; the master index; citation index; permutitle index; author index; research centre index. Volume 1, Part 2 has 187 pages.

The master index (65 pages in Volume 1, Part 2) is not cumulated. The entries identified by a running number contain the full details to which the other indexes refer. Each entry gives the author, title, journal title and full page references, or imprint and series title in the case of a monograph. This is followed by a full list of the books or articles cited in that book or article.

The subject approach is through the alphabetical 'permutitle' index, formed of keywords from the titles of articles. The author index shows all the instances in which that author's works have been cited in the books and articles indexed.

COVERAGE: Limited to Old Testament studies and ancient Near East studies, including appropriate theology, religion, archaeology, epigraphy, linguistics, history; and studies in individual countries such as Judaism, Assyriology, Egyptology. Material for indexing includes books, periodical articles, Festschriften, congress proceedings. It is drawn from all the languages and countries in which the subjects are discussed. The master index has 681 entries from about 300 periodicals.

COMMENT: Volume 1, Parts 1 & 2, index material from 1975 and 1976. They were published in 1978 and 1979 and appear to be later than was intended.

This guide sets out to do much more than the usual subject indexing service. In particular, it can lead into a qualitatively selected retrospective bibliography of the topic sought (assuming that authors only quote other articles if they think they are relevant, and good).

For a fuller assessment, see the review by G. R. Wittig in *Bulletin of the Association of British Theological and Philosophical Libraries* new series No. 15 (June 1979) pages 5–10.

Published by Infodex (Pty) Ltd., P.O. Box 2149, Stellenbosch 7600, Republic of South Africa

125 Ostkirchliche Studien
Vol. 1– ; 1952–
Quarterly   24 cm

ARRANGEMENT: Each issue contains articles, book reviews, occasionally a section listing the contents of Zeitschriften, and the Bibliographie. The Bibliographie is classified and appears over several years: thus the eight issues from May 1978 to December 1979 cover:

  I. Theologie.
     9. Hagiographie (continued).
     10. Ökumene.
  II. Philosophie und Literatur.
  III. Geschichte.
     1. Allgemeines (Sammelwerke und Zeitschriften, Handschriften, Bibliographien und Biographien).
     2. Spätantike, Byzanz, Griechenland.
        Kirchengeschichte.
        Kulturgeschichte und politische Geschichte.
     3. Russland und andere slavische Länder: Rumänien.
        Kirchengeschichte.
        Kulturgeschichte und politsche Geschichte.
     4. Orient:
        Kirchengeschichte, Kultur- und politische.

Within headings, the entries are arranged alphabetically by author. Each entry gives brief bibliographical details. There are author indexes at the end of each year.

COVERAGE: Periodicals, books and Zeitschriften in many languages are listed for their coverage of the Eastern Churches. Over 1200 items are listed annually.

COMMENT: The lack of detailed subject arrangement and the rather desultory appearance (up to six years, depending in part on which part of the classification happens to be covered) do not make this an easy work to use. Probably a work of last resort unless comprehensive coverage is needed.

Published by Augustinus Verlag, Grabenberg 2, 87
Würzburg, Federal Republic of Germany
ISSN 0030-6487

6 Pastoral Care and Counselling Abstracts
Vol. 1–   ; 1972–
Annual; no cumulations   28 cm

ARRANGEMENT: The 1978 volume has 76 pages of abstracts
and 18 pages of preliminary matter in duplicated typescript.
The main division of the abstracts is into those of
unpublished research and published research. A new
section was added in 1978 for research in progress. About
twenty subject headings are used to sub-divide the abstracts
in each section. Most abstracts are listed under more than
one subject heading. There is an author index and a list of
the subject headings used.

COVERAGE: Subjects covered are clinical pastoral education;
pastoral counselling, its theology, resources and methods;
applications of pastoral counselling in hospital work,
mental health, parish work, group counselling, marriage
and the family, alcohol and drugs, death and bereavement,
vocational choice, education, religious experience. The
published research is in the form of periodical articles (27 in
1978). There are 29 abstracts reporting unpublished work in
the same volume. All abstracts are of work in the U.S.A. and
all are in English.

COMMENT: The printed items referred to are all from the
year named in the title of each volume, which is published
early in the following year. It is not easy to find abstracts on
specific subjects, partly because of the somewhat random (to
a non-psychologist) arrangement of subject headings, and
partly because of the large type used and the generous
spread of material over the page. Nevertheless it is an
inexpensive source of information on recent work, and
work in progress, in the area where pastoral theology and
psychology overlap.

Published by The Joint Council on Research in Pastoral Care and Counseling, P.O. Box 5174, Richmond, Virginia 23220, U.S.A.

127 Philosophy East and West

A quarterly of Asian and comparative thought
Vol. 1– ; 1951–
Quarterly   25.5 cm

ARRANGEMENT: The section in question is known as Current Periodicals and in the periodical issues examined it covered between one and two pages, after the articles and book review section. Relevant periodicals are taken and their main articles listed. The periodicals are arranged in title order and within each periodical there is a chronological arrangement for each article. There is no pagination for the articles. There is no author/title index, and although there is an annual index, it does not include the articles mentioned in the Current Periodicals section.

COVERAGE: Articles listed are specifically within the field of oriental and comparative philosophy, except occasionally when a full table of contents is published to indicate the scope of a particular journal. The periodicals themselves come from several parts of the world – Great Britain, U.S.A., Italy, India, China, Japan. (Those from the latter two countries are translated for the list). The subjects covered include Buddhist, Hindu, Islamic and Taoist philosophies among others. Although the coverage is in the main given to philosophy and philosophical concepts, some articles on religions are included.

COMMENT: The section itself is not very large, although periodicals are taken from several parts of the world. The lack of any author index has been commented on. There are no annotations supplied with the articles, and the lack of page numbers means that the length of an article, and possibly its importance, cannot be ascertained.

Published by University Press of Hawaii, 2840 Kolowalo
Street, Honolulu, Hawaii, HI 96822, U.S.A.
ISSN 0031-8221

8   The Pope Speaks (TPS)
The Church documents quarterly
Vol. 1–   ; 1954–
Quarterly   23 cm

ARRANGEMENT: Following two to three pages of news and
notes the main body of each issue of *TPS* is devoted to
translations into English of texts of recent papal documents
(c. 80 pages). The relevant bibliographical section follows
this and is entitled, The TPS Log: a running list of Papal
Documents (c. 10 pages). This is a chronological listing of
Papal documents appearing in *L'Osservatore Romano (OR)*, the
official Vatican newspaper. Each entry has a running
number, title in English with the original in brackets, date
of the document, details as to its format, i.e., sermon, letter,
address, etc., to whom the document was addressed, the
number of words included in the document, the language
of the text, and finally, the date of the documents
appearance in *OR*.

COVERAGE: The subjects covered therefore are recent Papal
and other major Roman Catholic Documents.

COMMENT: In the issue examined there were 523 entries
covering the period November 1st 1978 – January 31st 1979,
and the issue itself was published in Spring 1979. The TPS
Log does therefore provide a reasonably up-to-date
documentation service. However, it is worth noting that
L'Osservatore Romano is available in an English edition and
that an annual index is provided. This index has a subject
arrangement while the TPS Log is in chronological order.

Published by Our Sunday Visitor Inc., 200 Noll Plaza,
Huntington, Indiana 46750, U.S.A.
ISSN 0032-4353

129 Psychological Abstracts (PA)

Non-evaluative summaries of the world's literature in psychology and related disciplines
Vol. 1– ; 1927–
Monthly; semi-annual expanded index   26 cm

ARRANGEMENT: Abstracts are listed under 16 major classification categories, some having sub-sections (64 in all) as shown in the table of contents to every issue. In addition to abstracts, there are some bibliographic citations or annotations covering books, secondary sources and articles peripherally relevant to psychology. The abstracts and citations are numbered consecutively. Within each heading, the abstracts are arranged alphabetically by author. An author and brief subject index appears in each issue which refer to the abstracts using the abstract number.

An expanded and integrated Volume Index is published every six months, of which the subject index covers some 1000 pages. Three-yearly cumulated indexes are also available. Further cumulations are published by G. K. Hall: *The Cumulated Subject Index to Psychological Abstracts, 1927–1960* (two volumes), is supplemented by three volumes covering 1961–1965, and two volumes covering 1966–1968. Author indexes are also available covering the years 1927–1972. The Thesaurus of Psychological Index Terms, (1977 edition) is well worth consulting for index terms and related headings.

COVERAGE: *Psychological Abstracts* is a major bibliographical enterprise. Over 950 journals, technical reports, monographs and other documents are scanned for material. Each semi-annual cumulated index (i.e. each volume) contains approximately 15,000 abstract records. There is a significant amount of religious material abstracted.

COMMENT: *Psychological Abstracts* is the most comprehensive abstracting service for psychology and, as such, should be an early resource for those interested in the psychological aspects of religion and religious behaviour. Since 1967, *PA* records are available on machine readable tapes which provide the basis for automated search and retrieval services known as Psychological Abstracts Information Service (PsycINFO).

Published by the American Psychological Association, 1200 17th Street, N.W., Washington, D.C. 20036, U.S.A.
ISSN 0033-2887

0 **Public Affairs Information Service Bulletin (PAIS)**
Vol. 1– ; 1914–
Twice a month; three quarterly cumulations plus an annual bound volume with author index (author index since 1977)   26 cm

ARRANGEMENT: The main index covers some 835 pages in the annual volume and arranges the entries alphabetically by subject headings. The entries give full bibliographical details such as titles, authors, dates, pagination, and contents notes or brief abstract where necessary. *See also* references direct one to related headings. A Key to Periodical References gives full details of title, publisher, price, etc., and the Directory of Publishers and Organizations gives details of the publishers of books and reports listed in the index. An author index appears in the annual volume in which the details are briefer. In the introductory matter are a note on PAIS selection policy, a detailed user's guide to the *PAIS Bulletin,* and a list of abbreviations. Carrollton Press publish *Cumulative Subject Index to the PAIS Annual Bulletin, 1915–1974.*
    Religious material is scattered throughout the alphabet from Amish to Vatican but is quite well linked by references. Church and its sub-headings account for about a third of the entries. Multiple entries occur for compound subjects.

COVERAGE: 'The *PAIS Bulletin* is an index to a selection of the best and most useful literature of the social sciences ...' (Preface). Some 1400 periodical articles are covered yearly, plus books, pamphlets, government and other official documents, yearbooks and directories published in English throughout the world. Material written in French, German,

Italian, Portuguese and Spanish appears in *PAIS Foreign Language Index* a counterpart of *PAIS Bulletin*. Religious material is covered only insofar as it relates to public policy. Thus out of a total of some 27,550 entries in the 1978 volume, only 72 entries (representing about 60 articles) were covered. The books indexed are based on the intake of New York Public Library, one of America's largest.

COMMENT: The material, as befitting a publication on current affairs, appears promptly. The 1978 volume (covering October 1977 to September 1978) appeared in May 1979 and generally represented material published in that period. *PAIS Bulletin* is available on-line via the Lockheed DIALOG system from 1977.

Of value only to those interested in contemporary affairs, and particularly to those relating to public policy, but given this restricted subject, it is a valuable resource for those journals and publications outside the mainstream religious indexes and abstracts.

Published by Public Affairs Information Service, Inc., Editorial and Business Office, 11 West 40th Street, New York, New York 10018, U.S.A.
ISSN 0033-3409

131 Quaker History

Vol. 1– ; 1902–
Formerly *Friends' Historical Association Bulletin*.
Semi-annual; cumulative index every five years; Volumes 1–55 in 10 volumes   23.5 cm

ARRANGEMENT: The bibliographical section is at the end of the periodical after the articles and book reviews. It is entitled Articles in Quaker Periodicals. In a 1975 issue, seven different periodicals (not listed in alphabetical order) are recorded, and relevant articles listed, to cover a period of about one year, ending three months or so before the periodical publication date. The articles cover more than one issue of each periodical. Volume, number, date are given, as well as page numbers, and a brief annotation of the articles is given.

COVERAGE: In the main, the articles concentrate on Quaker history, and historical personalities, although a few articles of more general interest are included, for example an article on Swedenborg, and another on the causes of the French Revolution. Modern aspects of Quakerism are generally not included. The periodicals recorded are major Quaker periodicals published in Great Britain and the United States.

COMMENT: A restricted subject coverage but a useful Quaker abstract. It covers the major periodicals but does not seem to aim at a comprehensive coverage of all periodicals both in this country and overseas. It is restricted to periodicals, and as far as can be ascertained, does not include annual cumulations of the index. An author/editor index would be very useful, both with each semi-annual edition, and at the end of each year.

Published by Friends Historical Library, Swarthmore College, Swarthmore, Pennsylvania 19081, U.S.A.
ISSN 0033-5053

2 Quarterly Index Islamicus (IndIsl)

Current books, articles and papers on Islamic Studies
Vol. 1–   ; 1977–
Index Islamicus 1906–1955: a catalogue of articles on Islamic subjects in periodicals and other collective publications, compiled by J. D. Pearson (1958) was the original publication, after which various supplements were published to cover the period 1956–1975. From 1977 onwards, the *Quarterly Index Islamicus* replaced the supplements. Appropriate issues of the *Quarterly* will be cumulated in a quinquennial supplement which will continue the previous series, and the entries will be classified in a manner similar to the previous supplements.
Quarterly; cumulations in a quinquennial supplement intended   23.5 cm

ARRANGEMENT: Items are entered in a classified arrangement by region, country or language, beginning with Islam in general and then proceeding through the Middle East in general, North Africa, the Arab countries of the Arabian Peninsula and the Fertile Crescent and Arabic, to Iranians, Afghanistan, Central Asia and Muslim India to Turks, Ottoman Turkish and Cyprus. The section for Islam is always divided by subject and these same divisions are also used for the regional sections if the amount of titles listed justifies it. These divisions are as follows: General; Religion/Theology; Law; Philosophy/History of Science; Art; Music/Theatre/Broadcasting; Useful Arts; Geography/Travel; Archaeology; Palaeography/Diplomatic/Archives; Epigraphy; Numismatics; Papyrology; Heraldry/Genealogy; History; Social Sciences; Sociology/Anthropology/Psychology; Economics; Political Science; Education; Language; Literature.

Each section is identified by a letter of the alphabet and each section is in turn divided into two sequences, one for books and one for articles. Entry within this arrangement is alphabetical by author. For the entries relating to periodical articles the following information is provided: title of article, periodical, volume, number and date, details of pagination. There is no general list of periodicals indexed. For the entries relating to books, the title of the book, publisher, date of publication and series entry are provided, but there are no details relating to pagination. In the final issue for each year, an index to authors is provided.

COVERAGE: Current books, articles and papers on Islamic studies are included. The subjects covered by the *Index* can best be ascertained by referring to the subject divisions used by the *Index* itself as are listed under the section entitled 'Arrangement' above. There is comprehensive coverage of Islamic Studies. Islamic science and technology are generally speaking excluded from the *Index*. Each issue extends over some 30 pages and includes some 750 entries. Material from most of the Western countries is included.

COMMENT: As the *Index* is now being published quarterly a more up-to-date service is being provided than previously.

On average, the time span between material being published and appearing in the *Index* is up to one year. Some of the book material takes slightly longer to appear. Once one is familiar with the arrangement of the *Index* it is relatively easy to use. It is the only index available which aims at such comprehensive coverage of Islamic Studies and as such provides a valuable reference tool for libraries.

Published by Mansell Publishing, 3 Bloomsbury Place, London WC1A 2QA, U.K.

ISSN 0308-7395

3 Questions Liturgiques (QLP)

Vol. 1– ; 1910–

Formerly *Questions Liturgiques et Paroissiales.*

Quarterly   25 cm

ARRANGEMENT: Most issues of this serious, but not over-heavy, journal contain a Bulletin de Littérature Liturgique in addition to three or four reasonably learned articles which are usually, but not invariably, written in French. The Bulletin is arranged under a variety of headings and sub-headings, but these vary from year to year. Named abstractors provide fairly brief summaries of the entries in the Bulletin, together with full bibliographical information. The abstracts, which are always in French, sometimes approximate to reviews. Entries are numbered consecutively throughout each year, and there is an annual index of authors.

COVERAGE: Only books are included in the Bulletin, and the major emphasis is the history and practice of the Roman Catholic liturgy, though works on the liturgy of the Orthodox, and other non-Roman Catholic Churches are occasionally included. Liturgy is understood very widely, and includes studies in the theology of the Mass, of prayer and of the sacraments, as well as works on catechetics. The selection of books is basically European and, in the nature of the case, mainly non-English language. It would not seem to be exhaustive.

COMMENT: This is a useful, but not an essential, listing of liturgical studies and texts. The Bulletin is kept fairly well up to date, most items included having appeared a year before their listing. The existence of the works listed might be discovered from other sources, the *Ephemerides Theologicae Lovanienses* (No. 23) for example, but no other compilation gives such competent summaries of the books' contents.

Published by Questions Liturgiques, Mechelsestraat 202, B-3000 Louvain, Belgium

134 Rassegna di Letteratura Tomistica (RLT)
Vol. 1– ; 1966–
Continues *Bulletin Thomiste* with a double numbering of each issue. Thus, Volume 1 of the *RLT* is Volume 13 of the (new series) of *Bulletin Thomiste* which itself began in 1924 as an offshoot from the *Revue Thomiste*.
Annual; no cumulations   25 cm

ARRANGEMENT: The organization of the *RLT* has remained basically unchanged since the first issue. Each issue is divided into the following sections: Historica Circa Personam S. Thomae; De Scriptis S. Thomae; Fontes et Antecedentia; Philosophia; Theologia; Thomas et Auctores Saec. XIII–XX and (from Volume 6 onwards) Lexica, Congressus, Miscellanea, Localia. Each of the seven sections is further divided under appropriate sub-headings. The Bibliographia Thomistica Critica is normally preceded by a preface and a list of abbreviations, and followed by a series of supplements, divided once more into seven sections, which update the material covered by each year of publication of the *RLT*. Each issue concludes with the usual index of authors, a subject index, and a list of contents. Being solely a bibliographical tool its size reflects the extent of material produced in any one year, and, for that matter, the extent to which it has been noticed. The shortest issue so far has contained 245 pages, the longest 661.

COVERAGE: Anything and everything connected with the study of Thomas Aquinas and with Thomism in general is included. Over 250 journals are the subject of investigation. Articles, book reviews and congresses are covered. The journals tend to be either European, North American or Latin American.

COMMENT: Each annual issue deals principally with the material published three years ago. Thus the 1979 issue was ready for distribution on March 31st, 1979, and covers material dated 1976. It also contains supplements which survey, year by year, material missed by previous issues. The 1979 issue, for example, has some 17 pages concerned with material published between 1966 and 1975 and which, for a variety of reasons, has only now been noted. The guide is simple to use, and, in its specialized field, remains unrivalled. It is relatively inexpensive, and its omission from the library of any institution which claims to deal seriously with theology and philosophy should be regarded as surprising.

Published by Herder Editrice e Libreria, Piazza Montecitorio 120, 00186 Roma, Italy

5 Recherches de Science Religieuse (RSR)
Vol. 1– ; 1910–
Quarterly; Tables générales 1910–1960 (1963)   24 cm

ARRANGEMENT: The principal contents are scholarly articles and Bulletins Critiques – short reviews in French of recent literature in specific groups of subjects. There are a few longer book reviews and lists of books received. In 1978, Bulletins Critiques were included in three of the four issues. Altogether they occupied 276 of the 648 pages.

Each Bulletin is signed by a French scholar in the appropriate subject field. It begins with detailed bibliographical lists of the books to be reviewed and a survey of study in the field since the previous Bulletin on the same subject. Each Bulletin is further subdivided by subject. There are annual indexes to the Bulletins and to the books noticed.

COVERAGE: Recent Bulletins have covered philosophy of religion; New Testament, Old Testament and intertestamental literature; history of medieval ideas; patristic theology; dogmatic theology; political theology; Protestant theology; Islam; Church history. A full conspectus of all the Bulletins from 1910–1960 by subject is contained in the volume of cumulated indexes. The Bulletins review only monographs. They have an interdenominational approach. In 1978, 178 books, chiefly in French, German, English, Italian and Spanish, were included. A high proportion were published in France.

COMMENT: Most of the books were reviewed within two or three years of publication. There are some exceptions where the survey is the first on the subject for a longer period.

This guide can only be used systematically when the annual indexes are available. But it is good for its comparative surveys of recent monograph literature. Its sponsors also publish the *Bulletin Signalétique* (No. 61) which indexes the corresponding periodical literature.

Published with the support of the Centre National de la Recherche Scientifique, by Recherches de Science Religieuse, 15 Rue Monsieur, 75007 Paris, France
ISSN 0034-1258

136 **Religion in Communist Lands**
Vol. 1– ; 1973–
Quarterly; no cumulations   23.5 cm

ARRANGEMENT: The bibliographical section is found at the end of each issue. The arrangement of the bibliography varies slightly from issue to issue (dependent on material available) but the general format seems to be: (a) Significant Rumanian press articles on religion and atheism; (b) Selected articles from official Rumanian religious publications; (c) Rumanian unofficial religious documentation; (d) Samizdat (self-published material) in Rumania; (e) Significant Soviet press articles on religion and atheism; (f) Selected articles from official Soviet religious publications; (g) Soviet unofficial religious documentation; (h) Samizdat in U.S.S.R. The same layout is followed for Czechoslovakian and Bulgarian material when available. The transliteration system in the Soviet section of the bibliography is based on the Russian spellings of names and places except in cases where the original language was in the Roman alphabet. It gives a good bibliographic description of each article whether it is from a periodical or newspaper or taken from a pamphlet, photocopy or unofficial document.

COVERAGE: The bibliography appears to deal with material on Rumania, U.S.S.R., Czechoslovakia and Bulgaria. It does not as yet cover Poland, Yugoslavia, Hungary, or East Germany or any non-European communist state (although in such sections of the periodical as For the Record the news coverage is world wide, not limited to Europe). One of the aims is to record as much material as possible produced within the country itself, either official or unofficial, to give a broad picture of the religious situation. Thus documents, pamphlets, samizdat material, photocopies are recorded as well as periodical articles and books. For much of the material abstracts are given. Coverage in the main seems devoted to the Christian Churches, (although there are occasional references to non-Christian religions such as Judaism and Islam). Churches dealt with include the Orthodox, Roman Catholic, non-conformist groups such as the Baptist Church, and evangelical churches such as the Pentecostal Church. Coverage seems quite well up to date, e.g. the Summer 1979 issue deals with the period December 1978 up to February 1979.

COMMENT: The coverage and work on the bibliography are of a high standard, and a lot of research must be done to produce so much unofficial and 'ephemeral' material. As yet no annual cumulative index has been produced, but one suspects that th   uld be difficult anyway due to the high proportion of   icial material that would need careful indexing. It   haps to be regretted that there is not a general section on religion in communist countries before each country is dealt with individually.

Published by Centre For The Study of Religion and Communism, Keston College, Heathfield Road, Keston, Kent, BR2 6BA, U.K.
ISSN 0307-5974.

137 Religion Index One: Periodicals (RIO)

A subject index to periodical literature, including an author-index with abstracts, and a book review index
Vol. 1– ; 1949/52–
Volumes 1–12 (1949/52–1975/76) published under the title *Index to Religious Periodical Literature (IRPL)*.
Semi-annual; every fourth issue a bound cumulation for two years   28 cm

ARRANGEMENT: As stated in the sub-title, each issue and cumulated volume is in three parts: subject index (327 pages), author index with abstracts (313 pages), and index to book reviews (115 pages) together with a full list of the periodicals indexed. Volume 13 (1977/78) totals 757 pages.

The subject index is arranged alphabetically (word by word) under specific subjects following the Library of Congress style. There are many cross-references. Under each heading the sequence is alphabetical by title of the articles indexed. The title is followed by author(s), then periodical title, reference and date (all abbreviated). The author index, arranged alphabetically, has been separate from the subject index since Volume 12. The abstracts, usually supplied by the author, were first included at the same time, and about half of the entries in the latest volume have them. The book review index is also arranged alphabetically by author of the book reviewed.

COVERAGE: Very wide subject range in Christian religion, Bible, theology and Church history, comparative religion, etc.

Periodical articles and book reviews are indexed as described above. Originally basically Protestant in outlook it now gives ecumenical treatment. The editors claim that Volume 13 has 24,377 subject entries, 10,300 author entries and 4208 abstracts from 210 periodical titles. The subject index entries and the great majority of the abstracts are in English. 'Preference is given to journals published in North American and to English language journals from other countries ... [But] 25% ... are all or in part, in Western European languages.'

COMMENT: Most articles are indexed within one year of publication.

The fragmentation of knowledge and ideas into alphabetically arranged specific headings is not conducive to a systematic review of related subjects. The alphabet is also strictly applied so that Bible (NT) Acts precedes Bible (NT) Gospels and of course precedes Bible (OT). It is nevertheless the most comprehensive, English-language, guide to current religious periodicals available. It is well worth the cost in any research library.

Published for the American Theological Library Association by Religion Index One: Periodicals, 5600 South Woodlawn, Chicago, Illinois 60637, U.S.A. ISSN 0149-8428

38 Religion Index Two: Multi-Author Works (RIT)
Vol. 1– ; 1976–
Annual bound volume   28 cm

ARRANGEMENT: The volume is in two main sequences, an alphabetical subject index and an author and editor index. They are preceded by a full bibliographical list of the titles of the volumes indexed, with the abbreviation used. The 1976 volume has 134 pages; 1977, 184 pages. The subject headings are followed by the titles of the articles listed in alphabetical order. After the title comes the name(s) of the author(s), then the abbreviation for book title, page references and date. The author and editor index lists in one sequence: (1) under editor, the title and full contents list of each volume indexed; and (2) the authors and titles of the articles contained.

COVERAGE: The same broad subject fields of religion and theology are covered as in *Religion Index One* (No. 137). The Index includes separately published scholarly works which are collections of articles or chapters by more than one author, whether Festschriften or not. The 1976 volume claims to index 241 books, with 3065 author and 4975 subject entries. For 1977 the figures are 306 books, 4186 author and 7748 subject entries. Works included are in English or Western European languages.

COMMENT: The 1976 volume indexes works published during that year. It was published in 1978. The 1977 volume, including a few late 1976 titles, was published early in 1979. The same observations on using the subject index apply as to *Religion Index One* (No. 137). This is a most helpful supplement to *RIO*, and fills a gap by indexing a form of publication otherwise only retrieved from citations in further articles in the same subject field.

Published for the American Theological Library Association by Religion Index Two: Multi-Author Works, 5600 South Woodlawn, Chicago, Illinois 60637, U.S.A. ISSN 0149-8436

139   Religious and Theological Abstracts (RTA)
Vol. 1– ; 1958–
Quarterly;   27.5 cm

ARRANGEMENT: Each issue covers some 60 pages and contains abstracts of articles from major religious periodicals. The abstracts are arranged in a classified order and there are five main sections: Biblical, Theological, Historical, Practical and Sociological. Each section is further subdivided and there is a clear table of classification at the beginning of each issue. Within each subdivision entries are arranged alphabetically by author. Full bibliographical details are provided and for each article entered there is a brief abstract (normally up to 100 words). The abstracts are all in English with a note at the end of each one indicating the language of the article. The initials of the abstractor are also given. Issue No. 4 of each volume contains the indexes for the whole volume. Each abstract is given a running number and the indexes refer to each entry by its number. A subject index, author index and scripture index are provided. Each article is classified according to its primary emphasis and the indexes enable the user to trace abstracts which might not be found readily in the general classification. A list of abstractors is also provided.

COVERAGE: *Religious and Theological Abstracts* is a non-sectarian publication and it is comprehensive in its coverage of religions and theology. The emphasis is towards Christianity although there are sections covering the other world religions. The five main subject divisions are broken down as follows: (1) Biblical – General, Languages, O.T. Intertestamental Period and N.T.; (2) Theological – Philosophy, Prolegomena, Dogmatics, History of Doctrine and Ethics; (3) Historical – History, Biography, Church History, Denominations, Ecumenics, Judaism, World Religions, Church & State; (4) Practical – The Ministry, Homiletics, Worship, Pastoral Care, Church Administration, Education, Mission, Religion and Culture; (5) Sociological – Sociology, Social Institutions, Social System, Social Processes.

A list of some 160 journals indexed is provided and each issue contains around 900 entries. Many of the journals are of American origin but the list includes major titles from all over the world.

COMMENT: It appears that articles take anything up to a year after publication before appearing in the index. As a reference tool, *Religious and Theological Abstracts* has several points in its favour. It is particularly useful to have abstracts for articles, and on the whole the publication is clearly set out and is easy to use. The various indexes at the end of each volume are very helpful. When the range of subjects covered by the publication is considered it is clearly a valuable addition to any library specializing in the subject field of religion.

Published by Religious and Theological Abstracts Inc., Myerstown, Pennsylvania 17067, U.S.A.
ISSN 0034-4044

140 Religious Reading

Religious reading: the annual guide
Vol. 1– ; 1973–
Annual

ARRANGEMENT: Arranges the year's religious books into broad subject chapters. These include: General Reference Books, The Bible, Theology, Spiritual Life, The Church, History and Biography, and Denominations and Sects. Subsections within the chapters highlight special topics such as books on sickness, aging and death, and personal religious experiences. For each book details are given of author, title, publisher, price, date of original publication in the case of reprints, and the name of the series in which the book appears. Annotations of 75 to 100 words are provided by the publisher of the book. There are author, title and publisher indexes.

COVERAGE: *Religious Reading* lists and describes between 1500 and 2000 new religious books each year. It is not a selective bibliography, but attempts a complete survey of religious literature from all American publishers, both commercial and church affiliated.

COMMENT: The coverage of *Religious Reading* largely duplicates the religious items in the *Subject Guide to Books in Print* (No. 163), but the different arrangement and the annotations would make this a more attractive item for specialist religious libraries, and for people wishing to know what recent American publications have appeared on particular subjects.

Published by Consortium Books, P.O. Box 9001, Wilmington, North Carolina 28401, U.S.A.

41 Religious Studies Review (RelStR)

A quarterly review of publications in the field of religion and related disciplines
Vol. 1– ; 1975–
Quarterly; no cumulations   28 cm

ARRANGEMENT: The *RelStR* is the American answer to the *Theologische Literaturzeitung* (No. 165) and the *Theologische Revue* (No. 166). It has much the same format, although the amount of space dedicated to review articles seems somewhat greater than in the German publications, and in the section entitled Notes on Recent Publications there is a very severe limit on the length of reviews. The Notes are followed by Recent Dissertations in Religion, listing completed theses undertaken in schools belonging to the Council on Graduate Studies in Religion, and Dissertations in Progress, listing approved titles of theses in the same schools, plus some others. There is an annual index of the books m̲   ̲ned in the 300 and more pages published in the c̲   a year.

COVER̲   ̲t from the listing of theses, only books are survey̲   ̲ournal. They are reviewed under a variety of hea̲   mparative Studies; Islam; South Asian Religio̲   ian Religions; Greco-Roman Religions; Judais̲m   ̲f European Christianity; Religion in North ̲   ̲aism in North America; Biblical and Related   ̲logy; Philosophy of Religion; Social-Scientifi̲c   ̲Religion; Psychology of Religion; Missiolog̲   ̲s, Literature and Religion. Books from all   ̲ld may be included, but the vast majority   ̲uage publications, and there is a strong An̲   ̲s has its advantages, for it makes the *RelStR*   ̲ful journal to watch for works on the indi̲   ̲s of North America, as well as for Judaism an̲   ̲ianity in that area.

COMMENT: Some 750 books are reviewed annually, a figure that is achieved only by a drastic limit being put to the number of words reviewers are allowed. Perhaps as a result the reviews vary widely in competence. The *RelStR* serves a useful role in making known, rather than in passing judgement upon, recent writing over the whole field of religious studies, and doing so within the covers of one reasonably inexpensive publication.

Published by Council on the Study of Religion, Wilfrid Laurier University, Waterloo, Ontario N2L 3C5, Canada
ISSN 0319-485X

142 Répertoire Bibliographique de la Philosophie (RBP)

Vol. 1– ; 1949–
Continues *Répertoire Bibliographique*, the supplement to *Revue Néoscolastique de Philosophie*, formerly the *Revue Néoscolastique*, which in 1946 became *Revue Philosophique de Louvain*.
Quarterly; no cumulations   24 cm

ARRANGEMENT: The first (February) issue of each year contains introductions, of two to three pages, in English, French, German, Italian and Spanish in which the purpose, coverage and arrangement of the *RBP* are set out in admirably clear language. The introductions are followed by a list of the periodicals covered, together with the abbreviations of their titles as used in this journal. Preceding the Répertoire is a useful outline of the organization of the journal. The second and third issues (appearing in May and August) contain only the Répertoire while the fourth issue (November) has a Répertoire des Comptes Rendus, indexes and list of contents. Volumes for the last ten years have contained, on average, in excess of 700 pages.

COVERAGE: For the most part, the *RBP* confines itself to philosophical literature published in Dutch, English, French, German, Italian, Latin, Portuguese, Spanish and Catalan, though occasionally work in other languages may be cited. It guarantees to list all articles which have been published in the journals mentioned in the first issue of each year, and articles in other journals may also be included, though not on a systematic basis. There is a note in the introduction pointing out that the term 'philosophical literature' is interpreted 'rather strictly' –

scientific disciplines related to philosophy, and the auxiliary sciences of philosophy and of the history of philosophy are not treated in their own right. These strictures apply particularly to symbolic logic, linguistics, psychology, aesthetics and theology. The list of books provided by the *RBP* is regarded by the publishers as exhaustive – a considerable claim, but apparently well-founded. The list of review articles published in the last issue for each year indicates the more important critical notices and review articles which have appeared in the c. 400 listed journals.

COMMENT: Of the 4039 books and articles cited in the first issue for 1979, the majority had appeared between 1976–1978, which is a fair guide to the currency of the *RBP*. The *RBP* is easy and pleasant to use, though the excellent introduction is obligatory reading. It is intelligently organized. The first section, devoted to the history of philosophy, is largely chronologically based while the second section on philosophy itself is divided into the various branches of the subject. There is a sub-division on the philosophy of religion, but those interested in religious studies will also find the *RBP* useful for its sub-divisions on the history of patristic and medieval philosophy, and on moral philosophy. The user suffers from being unable to make maximum benefit of the *RBP* until it is complete for one year, but this criticism apart, the *RBP* can be highly recommended.

Published by Éditions de l'Institut Supérieur de Philosophie, L'Université Catholique de Louvain, Louvain-la-Neuve, Belgium
ISSN 0034-4567

3 **Répertoire Bibliographique des Institutions Chrétienne / Bibliographical Repertory of Christian Institutions (RIC)**

Vol. 2– ; 1969–

Volume 1, entitled, in its English version, *Documentation, Computer and Christian Communities* by Marie Zimmermann, a general introduction to the series, appeared in 1974.

Semi-annual since 1977; annual from 1969–1976; no cumulations   24 cm

ARRANGEMENT: *RIC* is in two parts. The first contains the full bibliographical references, arranged by country, and the second a general index in English (of sorts) and indexes of the keywords in French, German, Spanish and Italian. A vital explanatory note is included at the beginning or at the end. The most recent issues of *RIC* have all contained over 300 pages, amounting to over 600 pages a year.

COVERAGE: It is very far from clear what the scope of this bibliography is meant to be. The general index lists some 850 English keywords from Abortion Christianity to Zen Christianity. But as the title of the *Répertoire* suggests, there appears to be a stress on the institutional aspects of Christianity, rather than on the personal and spiritual. Over 1000 periodicals are indexed, but from a limited number of countries. Europe is surveyed fairly thoroughly, Africa is treated as one country for the purpose of the index, and from outside Africa and Europe only the U.S.A. and Australia are covered. There would appear to be no denominational bias.

COMMENT: *RIC* is published in May and October, and the use of the computer reduces to a minimum the time-lag between an article appearing and its citation. Thus articles appearing in the second half of 1977 should be cited by the volume of *RIC* published in March 1978. But the computer brings with it numerous disadvantages. The English is quaint because it is quite clearly geared to French, despite the fact that English is the main language of the general index. The computer prints only in upper-case letters, making a page of type difficult to read. And although frequent use of *RIC* may make for (relatively) easy handling, the occasional user will find manipulating it extremely time-consuming. An Italian, for example, might look up 'regno di dio' in the Italian index. This refers him to entry No. 321, Kingdom of God/Royaume de Dieu in the general index, and to a list of numbers grouped from 3 to 1. The number 3 indicates that the article cited there is 'very

162

important', 2 that it is 'important' and 1 that it is 'interesting'. It would therefore seem at first glance that *RIC* is evaluative, but a note explains that '*the evaluative index* in no case constitutes a value judgment on the document concerned, but only a first classification to keep the reader from drowning in a flood of bibliography'. The general index refers the user to the bibliography-by-country section by means of a complex number, made up as follows: the first digit (in descending order from 3 to 0) indicates whether there is a bibliography, and, if so, of what standard; the second digit (from 0 to 9) indicates which religious denomination is being discussed in the article concerned; the third and fourth numbers – or rather, letters – represent the country in which the periodical was published, and the final four digits are the serial number of the entry under each country. Many entries in the general index have an additional indicator 'R' (related term) drawing the user's attention to another entry in the index. Given the complexities of use, unless very up-to-date information is required an enquirer would be better served by *Religion Index One* (No. 137), or by the rather less comprehensive *Catholic Literature and Periodical Index* (No. 69).

It should be noted that there is a series of Supplements to *RIC*, arranged on a thematic basis, and listing books as well as periodical articles.

Published by Cerdic Publications, 9, Place de l'Université, 67084 Strasbourg Cedex, France
ISSN 0079-9300

4 Répertoire des Thèses de Doctorat Européennes/ Belgique
Vol. 1– ; 1971/2–
Compiled from the Catalogue of European doctoral theses (i.e. *Répertoire des Thèses de Doctorat Européennes*)
Annual   21 cm

ARRANGEMENT: Arranged into three sections: (a) an alphabetical ordering of author's names followed by the title of their thesis in the original language – mostly French,

Flemish or English; (b) arranged into three major disciplines: Humanities, Medicine, and Science; (c) according to an alphabetical arrangement of keywords taken from each title, followed by the title and a serial number which refers back to the fuller entry in the author listing. Each thesis may be mentioned several times according to the various keywords in its title. The keywords are, of course, in the language of the thesis so users must beware variant spellings, for example, Marcus and Mark (St.), Theologie and Theology. Prefatory matter is given in English, Spanish, French and Flemish.

COVERAGE: Lists the titles and authors of theses submitted for doctorates in the Belgian universities during the previous academic year. About 650 theses are listed yearly. Subject coverage is wide, and while religious items form but a small part, items range from Biblical exegesis to liberation theology, and from the Church in Singapore to English Protestants in eighteenth-century Belgium.

COMMENTS: Coverage is that of the previous year with another year needed for publication. Application for theses must be made to the relevant universities, the addresses of which are given. Keyword indexes are rarely satisfactory for subject searching, but the quality of work done in these universities makes this index a useful and fairly easy work to use.

Published by the Ministère des Affaires Étrangères, 2 Rue des Quatre Brasstraat, Bruxelles, Belgium

45 Review of Religious Research (RRelRes)
Vol. 1– ; 1959/60–
Three a year; no cumulations, though there is an author/subject index to Volumes 1–20 (1959–1979)   23 cm

ARRANGEMENT: The first twenty years of *RRelRes* have been characterized by growth and also by changes in format and organization. As these variations have in no respect obscured the basic structure of the journal no comment is necessary here. Four divisions suggest themselves: original research articles and critiques of published research; abstracts of research articles published elsewhere, of dissertations, and of reports by organizations and individuals; book reviews; a bulletin of events and personal news of interest to members of the Religious Research Association – including obituaries coyly entitled Deaths in the Family. Of particular interest is the section now called Research, and Planning Abstracts. It is the product of a regular survey of professional journals, *Dissertation Abstracts International* (No. 78), and a number of Church agencies, together with abstracts of individual studies sent by their authors in response to an open invitation by the editor.

COVERAGE: The Religious Research Association considers itself to have a dual commitment to the advancement of scientific theory and research in religion, and to the concerns of religious leaders outside the academic community. *RRelRes* tries to maintain communication between those who study religion from various perspectives, and those whose daily decisions affect the future of religion as it is currently organized. Research is defined broadly to include any work which specifies a problem of religious concern, describes and analyses that problem in terms of causes and consequences, and considers the implications from organized religion and further research. While the scope of the journal would appear to be Religion in general, in practice most of the research tends to be in the fields of religious psychology and religious sociology. Books and book reviews are not covered in the abstracts section, though reviews of course occur elsewhere in the journal, but periodicals, reports and dissertations are. Abstracts of relevant dissertations result from *DAI* scans by the editor. Abstracts of individual and corporate research of interest appear to be obtained on a less systematic basis. The periodical literature data-base looks minute. This may be a reflection on the paucity of the literature in general, but in practice *DAI*, *Social Analysis* and the *Journal for the Scientific Study of Religion* have tended to contribute two-thirds of the abstract material. The remainder has come from another ten or so American journals, or is of non-periodical origin.

COMMENT: The average gap between original publication and appearance in *RRelRes* is about twelve months. The Research and Planning Abstracts is not difficult to use, but is likely to be of help only to sociologists and psychologists of religion, and thus recommend itself only to specialized libraries, though the subscription to the *Review of Religious Research* is really quite low.

Published by the Religious Research Association, P.O. Box 303, Manhattanville Station, New York, New York 10027, U.S.A.
ISSN 0034-673X

146 **Revista Agustiniana de Espiritualidad (RAE)**
Vol. 1– ; 1960–
Three issues a year; no cumulations   23.5 cm

ARRANGEMENT: Each issue – in practice only two a year, though the *RAE* claims three – contains about six articles on spiritual topics followed by book reviews and the Revista de Revistas de Espiritualidad. This last section is arranged current-contents style, alphabetically by title of the journal, with its contents listed beneath the title.

COVERAGE: The subject matter is spirituality in general, and the scope of the Revista de Revistas takes in approximately a hundred journals – books, obviously, are not included. Most of the titles listed are in either Portuguese or Spanish, but there are a few in French or German.

COMMENT: Much of the type of material covered by this Revista de Revistas cannot be found elsewhere, at least with any ease, so the *RAE* performs a useful function in drawing its readers' attention to the other periodicals. The currency, moreover, is excellent. In the volume for 1979, for example, the entries were either of journals published in the previous year, or even in 1979.

Published by Revista Agustiniana de Espiritualidad, Avenida de la Estación 9, Calahorra, Logroño, Spain

7 **Revue Bénédictine. Supplément: Bulletin d'Ancienne Littérature Chrétienne Latine / Bulletin de la Bible Latine (RBen: BALCL/BBL)**
Vol. 1– ; 1921–
Quarterly; no cumulations   25 cm

ARRANGEMENT: Fascicules of the *BALCL/BBL* appear irregularly, appended to the regular issues of the *Revue Bénédictine*. (The *RBen*, incidentally, though it claims to be a quarterly, in practice appears semi-annually.) These fascicules are paginated separately from the rest of the *RBen*, the page numbers being given in square brackets to distinguish them from the other supplement of the *RBen*, the *Bulletin d'Histoire Bénédictine* (No. 148), which has asterisks added to its page numbers. The Bulletin de la Bible Latine is theoretically a sub-series of the Bulletin d'Ancienne Littérature Chrétienne, but is all that, to date, has appeared of the *BALCL*. Of the *BALCL/BBL* five complete volumes have so far been published, and Volume 6 is advanced to the extent of 92 pages. Volume 5 consists of 326 pages, including the indexes. Each fascicule or *cycle* – Volume 5 contains seven of them – is organized under the following headings: Ensemble de la Bible; Ancien Testament; Nouveau Testament; Apocryphes; Canon, Sommaires, Prologues. At the end of *BALCL/BBL* are the indexes: modern authors; biblical citations; Latin manuscripts; Latin words; subjects.

COVERAGE: If it is not already clear it should be emphasized that the concern of the *BALCL/BBL* is the Latin Bible and nothing else. No list of periodicals has been provided, but there appear to be no significant gaps in what, it must be admitted, is a highly specialized and limited subject field. Progress in the major series – *Corpus Christianorum, Corpus Scriptorum Ecclesiasticorum Latinorum* or Lowe's *Codices Latini Antiquiores* for example – is followed. Each entry, consisting of a full description of the book or article and a comment upon it, is numbered. Volume 5 contains 847 entries, Volume 6, to date, has 248.

COMMENT: Currency is not impressive, but perhaps this is not a critical matter in this area of study. While each fascicule may be scanned fairly quickly, maximum exploitation of the literature is impossible without recourse to the indexes which, on past form, may well take ten years to appear. The fact that the two supplements are sewn into each issue of the *RBen* makes life difficult for the user. If *RBen* is bound annually the supplements should be taken out, which increases their vulnerability. If they are not removed, whether *RBen* is bound or not, then searching for, let alone through, the fascicules becomes very tedious. There would seem little point in purchasing the *RBen* for the *BALCL/BBL* alone. If the potential purchaser has little or no interest in Benedictine matters, which, after all, are the principal concern of the journal, purchase cannot be recommended.

Published by Abbaye de Maredsous, 5462 Maredsous, Belgium
ISSN 0035-0893 (for the *RBen*)

148 Revue Bénédictine. Supplément: Bulletin d'Histoire Bénédictine (RBen: BHB)
Vol. 1– ; 1907–
Quarterly; no cumulations   25 cm

ARRANGEMENT: The *BHB* appears irregularly as part of the quarterly (in practice semi-annual, see previous entry) *Revue Bénédictine*, and is paginated separately. Each volume of the *BHB* is organized under four main headings, with appropriate sub-headings: 'Saint Benoit et sa Règle'; 'Generalités'; 'Histoire des Monastères'; 'Biographies'. Nine volumes of the *BHB* have so far appeared, and Volume 10 is advanced to the extent of 176 pages. Volumes 8 and 9 had, respectively, 846 and 700 pages, and they took, again respectively, five and four years to complete. The final fascicule of each volume contains the author and subject indexes.

COVERAGE: The sole concern of the editor is the literature of the history of the Benedictines, and this is interpreted fairly strictly. No details of the data base are forthcoming, but no ominous gaps in the literature have been noticed. Indeed, a Sotheby's catalogue containing a book with a Benedictine provenance is noted in the latest volume. Each entry is numbered, and Volume 8 contained 5090 citations of books and periodical articles, while Volume 9 had 3813 entries.

COMMENT: While the *BHB* is obviously invaluable for those interested in the history of Benedictine monasticism, it suffers from all the disadvantages mentioned when discussing the *Bulletin d'Ancienne Littérature Chrétienne Latine/ Bulletin de la Bible Latine* (No. 147). So for further information see the previous entry.

Published by Abbaye de Maredsous, 5462 Maredsous, Belgium
ISSN 0035-0893 (for the *RBen*)

9 **Revue de Qumran (RdQ)**
Vol. 1– ; 1958–
Four issues per volume; but frequency varies   26 cm

ARRANGEMENT: From the outset each issue has consisted of a maximum of four sections: articles; notes; reviews; bibliography; though occasionally one or more of the sections, apart from the articles, may be missing from an individual issue. The Bibliographie continues, informally, from where Christoph Burchard's *Bibliographie zu den Handschriften vom Toten Meer* (Berlin: Töpelmann, 1957) left off. It appears in each of the first three issues of a volume. Its place in the fourth issue is taken by indexes to the volume. Each Bibliographie is divided in two, into books and periodicals, each of which sections is further sub-divided. The books are arranged under five headings: Ouvrages; Ouvrages Connexes; Ouvrages Collectifs; Rééditions ou Traductions and Thèses Manuscrites. The periodical section lists alphabetically by periodical title any item of interest. Each entry in the Bibliographie is numbered, the numbering starting anew with the beginning of each volume. The extent of the Bibliographie obviously reflects the literature of the subject, as does the publishing policy in general: the *RdQ* does not commit itself to a fixed number of issues per year, but promises to appear as soon as there is enough material to make up 160 pages. Volumes consist of about 650 pages, of which the bibliographical sections make up between ten to fifteen percent.

COVERAGE: Only scholarly literature on the Qumran community and the Dead Sea Scrolls is eligible for inclusion. No list of periodicals covered has been provided, but the geographical and linguistic range appear impressive. Books, book reviews and dissertations are included. Volume 9, for 1977–1978, contained 691 entries.

COMMENT: The currency is not particularly good. The editorial in the first issue of *RdQ* emphasized the importance of acquainting scholars with the latest developments as quickly as possible, but the journal has failed to deliver in this respect. Volume 9 took two years to complete, and even were the reader prepared to do without the indexes he would have found a considerable time gap between an article's first publication and its citation – the three Bibliographies contained in that volume concerned themselves for the most part with literature published between 1973–1976. While there is some attempt to organize the book material, the arrangement of the periodical section by journal title is not particularly helpful – what has been written is more important than where it is to be found, at least in the first instance. *RdQ* is well indexed, but a gap of two years from the first issue of the volume to the last one containing the indexes is too long. Imperfect as it is, however, it is unrivalled in its specialist coverage. Like so many specialist publications it is not particularly cheap.

Published by Gabalda, 90 Rue Bonaparte, 75006 Paris, France

Revue des Sciences Philosophiques et Théologiques (RSPhTh)

Vol. 1– ; 1907–
Quarterly; no cumulations   25 cm

ARRANGEMENT: Scholarly articles share the pages of each issue of this periodical with regular literature surveys (Bulletins); contents lists of recent periodical issues (Recension des Revues); and short book reviews (Notices Bibliographiques). Volumes have 600–700 pages. Each Bulletin is by a French scholar on one subject area, with substantial accounts of recent publications, giving full bibliographical listings (172 pages in 1977). The Recensions list the contents of each periodical issue, with brief annotations (102 pages in 1977). The Notices Bibliographiques (41 pages in 1977) are in no systematic order, but are indexed at the end of each volume, as are the Recensions and the Bulletin entries.

COVERAGE: Subjects surveyed in recent issues have been: in theology – Christology, Holy Spirit, the Virgin Mary, medieval doctrine; in philosophy – phenomenology, Teilhard studies; in history, etc. – ecclesiology, liturgy, patrology, Islam.
 Books and periodical articles are noted in the surveys. The coverage of the other sections is noted above. The *Revue* is produced by the Dominican Fathers of the Faculties of Theology and Philosophy at Le Saulchoir, Paris. The materials surveyed are from France, Germany and other European countries, with a considerable proportion of English language items. The surveys, notes on periodicals (about 100 titles), and book reviews are all in French.

COMMENT: Most of the items surveyed were published one or two years previously, except in subjects where a longer interval had elapsed since the previous survey. The current contents notes on periodicals were usually from the preceding twelve months. The volume of bibliographical information in the *Revue* is enormous, occupying about half the published pages. But its value from the systematic searcher's point of view is limited, unless a survey coincides with the subject sought.

Published with the support of the Centre National de la Recherche Scientifique, Librairie Philosophique J. Vrin, 6 Place de la Sorbonne, 75005 Paris, France
ISSN 0035-2209

151 Revue d'Histoire de la Spiritualité (RHS)

Vol. 1– ; 1920–
Publication temporarily suspended at the end of 1977.
1920–71 published as *Revue d'Ascétique et de Mystique (RAM)*.
Quarterly (but published as two double numbers 1975–1977); tables générales, 1920–1949; 1950–1960; 1961–1977
24 cm

ARRANGEMENT: Recent volumes have had about 400 pages of which the majority are devoted to scholarly articles. In 1977 there were also 7C pages of the Bulletin d'Histoire de la Spiritualité and 26 pages of book reviews. The Bulletin is in three sections, comprising literature-surveys by three different authors for the three periods (end of the Middle Ages; the modern period; the contemporary period), in the same style as in *Recherches de Science Religieuse* (No. 135). In previous years these literature surveys were on more specific subject areas, and from 1964–1976 there is an annual Bibliographie Française d'Histoire de la Spiritualité for the publications of the year before. These are classified indexes to books and periodical articles, with an author index. The books reviewed are indexed by the original author's name in the cumulated indexes.

COVERAGE: The subject matter is Christian spirituality, which has been defined as 'the Christian life lived with some intensity '. Included therefore are all the works of writers of all periods who have dealt with the individual or corporate attempt to become closer to God, and all critical and historical writing about them. Mysticism, and some aspects of monasticism and religious orders are included also.

The Bibliographie covers periodical articles and books. The number of entries varies from 300 to 600. It is explicitly limited to the publications of French-speaking countries, and is not annotated.

COMMENT: The items listed were published in the year prior to listing. The Bibliographie is available as a separate pamphlet, but is not cumulated. The Bulletins d'Histoire de la Spiritualité are useful literature surveys, but have not continued long enough to be an important source of information.

Published (in 1977 with the support of the Centre National de la Recherche Scientifique) Revue d'Histoire de la Spiritualité, 15 Rue Monsieur, F-75007 Paris, France

2 Revue d'Histoire Ecclésiastique (RHE)
Vol. 1– ; 1900–
Quarterly   25 cm

ARRANGEMENT: The *RHE* is a scholarly journal covering all aspects of ecclesiastical history, though its emphasis, for the Post-Reformation period, is undoubtedly Roman Catholic. In addition to the three to four articles published in each number, about a quarter of the space is taken up by book reviews, and there is an even larger section entitled Chronique which, under a heading for each country, records current events, personalities and publications of interest to Church historians. The Chronique is followed by the Bibliographie, but this latter is paginated independently of the remainder of each issue, and is intended to be bound as a separate volume, made up over the year. A title-page for the Bibliographie volume is supplied. The Bibliographie has formed a distinct part of the *RHE* since 1903, and currently amounts to about 800 pages a year – the main body of the periodical reaching 900 pages or so. The bibliography is divided into four main sections: I. Auxiliary Sciences (bibliography, palaeography, methodology and so on); II. Sources and Criticism of Sources; III. Historical

Works 'Properly so Called'; IV. Citations of Reviews of those books which have already been listed. Each of these sections is further broken down. Section III, for example, is divided by period and by place, and includes liturgy, hagiography, the history of art and so on. The latest volume contains well over 11,000 citations of books and articles. Under each separate heading books are listed first, and then articles, each arranged in alphabetical order of author.

COVERAGE: The range of the *RHE* is enormous. It takes in anything that might in any way be considered Church history, and may, therefore, be consulted to find recent works on the New Testament – but not on the Old. Over a thousand journals are scanned, in addition to the innumerable books, and the 'catchment area' is world wide, although there is an understandable Western European bias, given the nature of the subject. Many of the periodicals included are neither historical or ecclesiastical, but are of the sort that may occasionally contain items of interest.

COMMENT: The full range of the bibliographical section of the *RHE* is published in each issue, which means that in any given year a researcher has to look in several different places for possible citations on his chosen topic. The burden is eased, however, by the fact that although the *RHE* claims to be quarterly it in practice appears only three times a year. The organization of the bibliography, its presentation and its currency are all outstanding. Items can indeed sometimes be missed, and included a couple of years late, but in comparison with other bibliographies, the failure rate is small. The majority of citations are dated to the year before inclusion in the bibliography. An additional advantage is that reviews of books are noted when possible at the same time as the book itself is cited, though as mentioned a moment ago there is also a section for reviews of books cited earlier. For what it offers the *RHE* is remarkably cheap, and no library that concerns itself with Church history and more especially the history of the Roman Catholic Church can afford to be without it.

Published by Bibliothèque de l'Université, Université Catholique, Place Mgr. Ladeuze, 3000 Louvain, Belgium
ISSN 0035-2381

53   Revue Théologique de Louvain (RTL)

Vol. 1– ; 1970–
Quarterly; no cumulations   24 cm

ARRANGEMENT: The *Revue* comprises scholarly articles, book reviews, bibliographical notes, chroniques, Chronique Louvaniste and Index International des Dissertations Doctorales en Théologie et en Droit Canonique Présentées en ... The first issue of the Index was published in Volume 9 (1978) pages 479–523, covering 1977, and also circulated as an offprint. Volume 9 as a whole has 530 pages. Entries in the Index are arranged in classified subject order preceded by an editorial note on the collection of the information; a list of subject headings; a list of abbreviations; and an index to the institutions for which the theses were written. Each main entry is identified by a running number, which allows reference from the institution and from additional brief entries under secondary subject entries. Abbreviations at the end of each entry show whether it has been published, or where an abstract may be read, or how the thesis may be consulted.

In each volume there are also 60 pages of book reviews, and 30 pages of notices (briefer comments), which are not arranged systematically but are listed in the annual indexes.

COVERAGE: The following subjects are covered: Bible; ecclesiastical history; all aspects of theology and religion; Canon Law; Church and State. Theses from Roman Catholic institutions seem to be more completely reported than from those of other traditions. Only 49 of 300 institutions responded to the questionnaire, providing entries for 292 theses. The languages in which the theses were written include English, French, German, Spanish, Italian, also Polish and Dutch with English or French or German translations of the title added. Most of the theses were reported from continental Europe and the U.K.; those from the U.S.A. were under represented.

COMMENT: All the theses reported in 1978 were submitted in 1977.

Published by Revue Théologique de Louvain, 1348 Ottignies-Louvain-la-Neuve, Belgium

154 Rivista Liturgica (RivLi)

Vol. 1–   ; 1914/15–
Six a year   20 cm

ARRANGEMENT: The individual issues of this periodical are regularly devoted to a single theme, and the last issue of each year is the bibliography. In addition to the bibliography, however, a Review of Reviews appears several times a year, and so do bibliographical surveys of particular topics. Church documents, official and semi-official, to do with the liturgy are also printed. Editorial policy seems at the time of writing to be in a state of flux, and it is a little difficult to give a clear indication of the journal's layout, and of the precise limits of the bibliographical information contained in the RivLi. The Review of Reviews and the bibliography both take the form of extended – sometimes quite lengthy – abstracts of books and articles. The names of the abstractors are indicated.

COVERAGE: The bibliography contained in the final issue of each year has usually been devoted exclusively to books. In 1979, however, it contained entries for reviews as well, in addition to the Review of Reviews section of each issue. Rather less than 150 journals are searched, some of them fairly obscure. There are one or two from the Americas, but the majority are Western European. The RivLi's concern is almost exclusively with Roman Catholic liturgy, and even within that field its especial interests are more practical than scholarly. The bibliography is divided into a number of sections, but the exact organization of these appears to vary from year to year. There is an excellent systematic index to the subjects covered, as well as one of authors cited.

COMMENT: Currency could not be described as better than fair. In the 1978 volume entries dated 1976 were about as frequent as those for 1977, and there was at least one dated 1970. Its spread of periodicals scanned is very far from being world wide, and its terms of reference are fairly narrow, but apart from these drawbacks, and the fact that everything is in Italian, the *RivLi* performs a useful function in providing lengthy abstracts of articles which originally appeared in out-of-the-way periodicals, which may be difficult to obtain.

Published by Centro Catechistico Salesiano, 10096 Leumann, Turin, Italy
ISSN 0035-6956

A Science of Religion

Abstracts and index of recent articles
Vol. 1–   ; 1976–
Formerly (1976–1979) *Science of Religion Bulletin: abstracts and index of recent articles*. It replaces *International Bibliography of the History of Religions* (No. 100).
Quarterly   29 cm

ARRANGEMENT: Each quarterly issue is divided into broad subject groupings. The exact description of the subjects varies a little from time to time, the latest being: General and comparative; Anthropology/Psychology/Sociology of Religion; Islam; Asian religions (except Islam); Greco-Roman antiquity; Ancient Middle East/Judaism.
The last issue every year has cumulated Author and Subject Indexes for all previous issues: thus the last issue of 1979 had indexes covering 1976 to 1979. The subject indexing is quite specific. The abstracts are full and average half the A3 sized page; they are signed, give adequate bibliographical details and are given a running number for indexing purposes. The abstracts are in English and many have been translated from Dutch, French and German originals (occasionally other languages).

COVERAGE: 'The object of the *Science of Religion Bulletin* is to provide a systematic bibliography of articles contributing to

177

the academic study of religion, with a view to facilitating the international collaboration of all scholars whose work has a bearing on the subject.' (Editorial matter). The title and note of arrangement above indicate the general subject field. Biblical studies and Christian material are generally omitted. Annuals and less frequently issued volumes are likewise excluded. Some 237 journals from all over the world are covered, from highly specialized ones to more general and regional ones. Many languages are covered. About 600 abstracts are presented yearly with a total of 2058 to date.

COMMENT: The full-sized typescript and large format, plus the generously full abstracts make for a pleasant appearance and easy reading. Coverage is wide and international. The broad subject fields are useful for general browsing and current awareness, while the cumulated and close classification of the subject indexes make for speedy retrieval. In general, it is a highly useful publication for those interested in religion and religions. The two-year delay between journal issue and abstract publication is a drawback.

Published by the Institute for the Study of Religion, Free University, Amsterdam, The Netherlands and the Department of Theology and Religious Studies, University of Leeds, U.K. Obtainable from Administration *Science of Religion*, The Institute for the Study of Religion, Free University, P.O. Box 7161, 1007 MC Amsterdam, The Netherlands.

155 Scriptorium (Scr)

Revue internationale des études relatives aux manuscrits/ International review of manuscript studies
Vol. 1– ; 1946/7–
Semi-annual: no cumulations   27 cm

ARRANGEMENT: *Scr* normally consists of four sections: articles; notes; Chronique and Bibliographie. The last-named is the focus of attention here, and in particular the

Bulletin Codicologique which, together with the Comptes Rendus, make up the Bibliographie. The Bulletin appears at the end of each issue, and is distinguished by a separate pagination which, as with the numbering of the entries, is cumulative for the volume. In addition the second issue of each volume contains a comprehensive index. A volume is likely to contain over 350 pages of text and some 250 pages of the Bulletin and its index. There are over a thousand entries, in a single alphabetical sequence by author or title. Each entry contains a full bibliographical description of the item, plus a brief review of the contents.

COVERAGE: A list of compilers for the Bulletin is provided, but not a list of the sources from which it is culled, so it is not possible to comment on the quality or extent of the data base with any degree of ease. Nor does any statement of publishing policy exist for the guidance of the user. All that can be said is that the coverage looks impressive, and that there is a considerable amount of material of interest to the Church historian and theologian. Books and periodical articles are included, but dissertations and reports are only likely to be noted if they are covered at a secondary level. The compilers are European or North American, as is their material.

COMMENT: Currency is not particularly impressive. Most of the entries seem to originate from one to two years before the publication of *Scr*, but there is usually a fair sprinkling of earlier material. But perhaps, in the field of manuscript studies currency is not such a high priority. No subject approach to the literature is possible, either via the organization of the Bulletin or by the index. In its more than thirty years of publishing history *Scr* has achieved a prominent position in its field. While as a bibliographical tool it could be better organized and is expensive, it has to be taken seriously as an aid to the researcher in early and medieval Christianity.

Published by Éditions Scientifiques, 8, P. van Duyseplein, 9000 Gent, Belgium
ISSN 0036-9772

156 Sefarad (Sef)

Revista del Instituto Arias Montano de Estudios Hebraicos,
Sefardies y de Oriente Próximo
Vol. 1–   ; 1941–
Semi-annual   24 cm

ARRANGEMENT: Each issue contains several scholarly articles,
which may be in most of the European languages, and in
Hebrew, followed by the Elenco de Articulos de Revistas.
The Elenco is itself arranged current-contents fashion, by
journal title and then the contents of each listed below.

COVERAGE: Some fifty journals, selected on a world-wide
basis for their interest in Jewish and Near-Eastern studies,
are listed in the Elenco.

COMMENT: It appears to be the practice often to list several
volumes of a periodical at one time, so the currency is very
bad indeed, especially for a 'current-awareness' type
publication. Thus the 1976 volume contained material from
as far back as 1972, and the 1977 volume, which was
published as a Festschrift, did not figure the Elenco at all.
Researchers would be well advised to look elsewhere for
assistance in searching out material on Jewish studies, to the
Index of Articles on Jewish Studies (No. 91), for example.

Published by Consejo Superior de Investigaciones
Científicas, Duque de Medicaneli 4, Madrid, Spain
ISSN 0037-0894

157 Seventh Day Adventist Periodical Index

Vol. 1–   ; 1972–
Semi-annual   25.5 cm

ARRANGEMENT: A straightforward alphabetical list,
dictionary-fashion, with Library of Congress subject-
headings. Entries give only the briefest information –
author, title, and a much abbreviated journal title, followed
by volume, part, date and page references.

COVERAGE: The coverage is limited to material of
'denominational interest'. In practice this means the *Index* is

limited to journals published by Seventh-Day Adventist institutions, although a few articles from non-Seventh-Day Adventist sources do sometimes find their way in. About 55 journals are indexed, reviews of books and letters to the editor being included. The introduction claims to cover one 'foreign' journal, which presumably means one non-English-language journal, since publications from the United Kingdom and Australia are included, as well as those from the United States.

COMMENT: Like other expressly denominational indexes, this one has a preponderance of items from not very scholarly publications. Of the 55 journal titles mentioned, 29 are only indexed selectively. The *Index* is useful for studying a denomination with pronounced views on many matters, and it is rather more satisfactory than some of its counterparts from other denominations.

Published by Loma Linda University Libraries, Loma Linda, California 92354, U.S.A.

58 **The Sixteenth Century Journal (SCJ)**
A journal for renaissance and reformation students and scholars
Vol. 1– ; 1970–
Semi-annual, occasional supplements   23 cm

ARRANGEMENT: Each issue comprises scholarly articles, review articles, book reviews and book notices. The book notices are lists of recent publications sent to the editor. Each volume of about 130 pages contains some 50 pages of book reviews, which are not arranged in any particular order.

COVERAGE: The subject area is the whole field of the European cultural renaissance and reformation of religion. Books (only) in European languages are reviewed, in English. The reviews cover about 40 books a year in considerable depth.

COMMENT: Most books are reviewed within one or two years

of publication. This is not a systematic nor extensive bibliography, but a good sample of significant new books for scholars in the field.

Published by The Sixteenth Century Journal, LB 115, Northeast Missouri State University, Kirksville, Missouri 63501, U.S.A.
ISSN 0361-0160

159 **Social Compass (SocComp)**
International review of the sociology of religion
Vol. 1– ; 1953–
Quarterly   24 cm

ARRANGEMENT: Each issue of this learned journal is usually devoted to a single theme, and the number of articles varies. Reports of conferences and other meetings are regularly featured. The bibliographical information proper occupies little space, only some 20 pages in well over 500 in the volume for 1979. It generally appears in the second issue of the year, and covers the year previous. It is endowed with the title International Bibliography of Sociology of Religion.

COVERAGE: The editors describe their bibliography as a 'systematic indexing only of specialized reviews (and not of books)'. These 'specialized reviews' number some 125, and are drawn almost entirely from Western Europe, and from North and South America. It is not quite clear how specialized is 'specialized': not all the journals cited are exclusively concerned with sociology or, indeed, entirely devoted to religion.

COMMENT: The bibliography is reasonably well laid out under a series of headings and sub-headings, each of which is given both in English and French. The headings are all allotted a number, and appear every year even if no entry is assigned to that number. Individual items indexed are entered in alphabetical order of author, and are not numbered. The currency is reasonable – by far the largest proportion of the citations having been published in the year prior to the year of publication of the bibliography, though some may turn up from earlier years. There is no index of authors or subjects to guide the researcher, and the amount of information given for each entry is the barest minimum – author, title and bibliographical reference. It is a useful bibliographical tool in its own way, but one suspects that with very little effort it could be a great deal better. Its main competitors in its field are of more general scope – the *International Bibliography of Sociology* (No. 99), for example.

Published by Social Compass, Place Montesquieu 1/boîte 21, B-1348 Ottignies, Louvain-la-Neuve, Belgium
ISSN 0037-7686

0 Social Sciences Index

Vol. 1–   ; 1974/5–
Continues in part the *Social Sciences and Humanities Index* (1965–1974) and *International Index* (1907–1965). A companion volume to the *Humanities Index* (No. 90).
Quarterly; annual cumulations   26 cm

ARRANGEMENT: Comprises an author and subject index to periodical articles arranged alphabetically by subject headings and authors. The entries give the author, article title, publishing details and pagination of the article indexed. The subject headings and sub-headings are quite specific and there are numerous *see* and *see also* references. An example is:

Great Britain
  Religion
    see also Pentecostal churches in Great Britain

A separate section of book reviews appears at the end of each issue and is arranged in alphabetical order of authors.

COVERAGE: Subject coverage is anthropology, area studies, economics, environmental science, geography, law and criminology, medical sciences, political science, psychology, public administration and related subjects. In the 1978 annual volume, the index covered 1031 pages and the book review listing covered 110 pages. 268 periodicals are indexed with an emphasis on North America. Although no mainstream religious journals are indexed, there are sufficient entries relating to religious topics to be considered here. The headings for Religion, Religions and Religious and their sub-headings in the 1978 volume listed 47 items and 73 *see* and *see also* references.

COMMENT: The quarterly issues generally relate to the previous six months while the annual cumulation is published some nine months in arrears. *Social Sciences Index* is useful for its wide coverage of journals which carry occasional articles on religious subjects in the social science area. The companion series *Humanities Index* (No. 90) covers religion in general.

Published by the H. W. Wilson Company, 950 University Avenue, Bronx, New York 10452, U.S.A.
ISSN 0094-4920

161 Sociological Abstracts

Vol. 1–   ; 1952/3–
Frequency varies; but currently five issues per year; yearly cumulative index issue published within nine months of the last issue (being the sixth issue of the volume)   28 cm

ARRANGEMENT: Each issue is arranged in 30 broad subject groupings, further divided into 63 narrower ones. The abstracts are of a paragraph in length, give full bibliographical details, and are arranged alphabetically by author within each subject grouping. Each abstract has a serial number which is used for reference purposes. Most issues carry one or more supplements covering papers read at conferences and meetings of sociological societies. These are numbered differently. Each issue carries its own Subject Index, e.g.: Religion (20–30 items per issue), Theology, Taoism, Clergy, Author Index and Periodicals Index, with details of all issues which have been abstracted. The *ISA Bulletin* (International Sociological Association) and other professional and advertising material is also included in some issues.

The *Index Issue* contains a Cumulative Subject Index, a Cumulative Author Index (with a separate one for the Supplements) and a Cumulative Periodical Index (which gives full publishing details of all journals covered – about 50 pages). The Cumulative Subject Index is particularly detailed in giving each abstract one or more entries with a fully descriptive index entry. The abstract number follows the entry.

COVERAGE: *Sociological Abstracts* is a classified abstracting journal covering a broad range of sociological articles in various languages. Over a thousand abstracts are based on non English language publications. The 1977 *Index Issue* carried 8267 abstracts of which 7061 were from serial publications and 1206 were abstracts from papers presented at various meetings. The Cumulative Subject Index covered 550 pages and had some 200 entries for Religion -s -ous. Other examples are Holy – three entries; Hebrew – one; Hasidism – one; God – three; and Glossolalia – two. Specialist religious journals covered included *Church History*, *Review of Religious Research* and *Journal for the Scientific Study of Religion*.

COMMENT: A complex and difficult item to handle, but comprehensive in its subject field and well served by a detailed subject index. For anyone at all interested in the sociological aspects of religion, *Sociological Abstracts* will be an extremely useful aid.

Published by Sociological Abstracts Inc., P.O. Box 22206, San Diego, California 92122, U.S.A.
ISSN 0038-0202

2 **Southern Baptist Periodical Index**
Vol. 1– ; 1965–
Annual   27.5 cm

ARRANGEMENT: The bibliography is set out in a dictionary format. Entries give no more than the basic bibliographical information needed to trace them.

COVERAGE: This is limited to the 15 journals of the agencies of the Southern Baptist Convention. Non-agency materials are indexed each year in the October issue of *Baptist History and Heritage* (BHHe).

COMMENT: The currency of this *Index* is excellent, appearing as it does only three to four months after the year to which it refers. As the title indicates, only journals are covered, but these are indexed exhaustively – even photographs are included. Much of the material, however, is of purely local interest and references are not easy to decipher. For scholarly items the bibliography published by the same Historical Commission of the Southern Baptist Convention in *BHHe* is much more useful. Although the *BHHe* is mainly limited to American publications it does include some English material, mostly from *The Baptist Quarterly*. Compared to the 320 pages of the 1978 edition of the *Southern Baptist Periodical Index*, the *BHHe* had only three pages in its October 1978 issue. They were, however, generally more useful to scholars.

Published by Historical Commission of the Southern Baptist Convention, 127 Ninth Avenue N., Nashville, Tennessee 37219, U.S.A.
ISSN 0081-3028

163 Subject Guide to Books in Print
The available books, new and old, in 62,000 subject categories with full ordering information
Annual   28 cm

ARRANGEMENT: Arrangement is alphabetically by subject heading, thence alphabetically or chronologically by sub-heading, and then alphabetically within each heading by the author (or title) of the books listed. In the 1978/79 edition, there are some 62,000 subject headings with over 53,000 cross-references. The headings and cross-references are selected from the eighth edition of *Library of Congress Subject Headings* and its supplements. The books included may be listed under more than one heading. Headings are explicit rather than general, e.g.

Church History (164 entries with 24 cross-references and
   scope note)
—Bibliography (2 entries)
—Chronology (a *see* reference only)
—Dictionaries (2 entries)
—Historiography (6 entries)
—Juvenile Literature (6 entries)
—Philosophy (2 entries)
—Primitive and Early Church, ca. 30–600 (8 cross-
   references and 51 entries)
—Fiction (2 entries)
—Middle Ages, 600–1500 (11 cross-references and 41
   entries)
—Historiography (1 entry)
—Reformation, 1517–1648 (a *see* reference only)
—Sources (1 cross-reference and 13 entries)
—Modern Period, 1500– (5 cross-references and 17
   entries)
—18th Century (1 cross-reference and 6 entries)
—19th Century (2 entries)
—20th Century (4 entries)

There is a useful introductory section and a 100-page list of
publishers. The information included in the entry covers
author, title, volumes, editions, Library of Congress
number, series information, language if not English, if
illustrated, price, ISBN and publisher.

COVERAGE: *The Subject Guide to Books in Print* lists some 425,000
books (in 1978/79 volume) which were in print and
published and distributed in the United States. Fiction,
poetry, drama, government publications and standard
versions of the Bible in English are generally omitted. The
number of works specifically or partially on religion is hard
to estimate, but is bound to be substantial.

COMMENT: Although not by any means restricted to
'current' books, the majority will certainly be of 'recent'
origin, while those less recent will tend to be the 'classics' or
'standards' that publishers consider to be of continuing
value. A companion work is *Subject Guide to Forthcoming Books*

which is a bi-monthly listing by subject of all books due to appear in the coming five-month period. No evaluative comments are provided, the *Subject Guide to Books in Print* being purely a listing with full publishing details aimed, primarily, at the book trade itself. Obviously books not in print are excluded. Despite these drawbacks, such a comprehensive listing with close subject indexing is a useful resource for subject searching: many of the items will be too recent to have been covered by other indexes and bibliographies, and obviously, the fact that all the items listed are in print will be relevant for those selecting books for libraries and reading lists. Although restricted to books available in the U.S.A., a large number of British publications are listed due to their being distributed by American agents. For a listing of books published in the United States each arranged by the Dewey Decimal Classification, see *American Book Publishing Record Annual Cumulative*. The *Subject Guide* is expensive, but is likely to be found in most large libraries, frequently hidden away in library offices.

Published by R. R. Bowker Company, 1180 Avenue of the Americas, New York 10036, U.S.A.
ISSN 0000-0159

164 Teología y Vida (TyV)
Vol. 1–   ; 1960–
Quarterly: no cumulations   24 cm

ARRANGEMENT: Each issue of *TyV* contains several articles, followed by a section entitled Noticias de Revistas Latinoamericanas, organized by journal title. For most of the articles listed an abstract is provided.

COVERAGE: The scope of the Noticias is very limited: it is interested only in theological, and perhaps general religious, periodicals published in Latin America. As a result, in any one issue of *TyV* only some two dozen periodicals are listed with their contents, and all of them, of course, are from Latin America.

COMMENT: Production of the Noticias is very rapid. The 1979 issues listed for the most part 1978, and some 1979, publications with their contents. It is a useful source of information about material which is not generally accessible, but for a straightforward bibliography, without the occasional abstracts, the *Bibliografía Teológica Comentada* (No. 33) should, perhaps, be preferred.

Published by Universidad Católica de Chile, Facultad de Teologia, Av. Bernardo O'Higgins, 340, Casilla 114-D, Santiago, Chile
ISSN 0049-3449

5 Theologische Literaturzeitung (THLZ)
Monatsschrift für das gesamte Gebiet der Theologie und Religionswissenschaft
Vols. 1–69; 72–   ; 1876–1944; 1947–
Volumes 70–71, 1945–1946 not published. Also *Bibliographisches Beiblatt, 1921–1942.*
Monthly; no cumulations, but detailed annual indexes to books reviewed, subjects surveyed and periodicals indexed   30 cm

ARRANGEMENT: Each issue has one scholarly article, followed by book reviews under systematic subject headings. Under each heading are only one or two reviews, but these are usually followed by a list of further recent books and periodical articles in the same subject area (which are not reviewed). There are also reviews of academic dissertations, author bibliographies (as birthday tributes), and current contents lists of periodicals. Each volume has about 450 pages (actually numbered by columns, two to a page).

COVERAGE: The subjects covered are: Religion in general; philosophy of religion; Biblical studies; Church history (especially local German Church history); systematic theology; creeds and confessions; ethics; religious education; mission; religious sociology, psychology, art, and literature.
Books, dissertations and periodical articles are covered,

189

mainly from a Protestant viewpoint. There are about 550 books reviewed in the 1978 volume. Very many more titles are listed but not reviewed nor included in the index. The very large number of periodical articles listed, either in current contents or in the subject sections, are not included in the general indexes either. The materials reviewed and indexed are drawn from Germany, France, Britain and other European countries, but all reviews and other matter are in German.

COMMENT: Books reviewed were published from one to four years before the reviews appeared.

This great-grandfather of theological indexing services is conducted entirely in German, and, as it always has been, from Leipzig. Nevertheless it numbers scholars from both the Federal Republic and the Democratic Repulic among its contributors. For German theology and Bible studies, and for the German view of non-German theology, it is indispensable.

Published by Evangelische Verlagsanstalt G.m.b.H., 701 Leipzig, Scherlstrasse 2, PSF 448, Berlin, German Democratic Republic
ISSN 0040-5671

166 Theologische Revue (ThRv)
Vol. 1– ; 1902–
Six a year   29.5 cm

ARRANGEMENT: The *ThRv* is edited by members of the Roman Catholic theological faculty of the University of Münster and is, in effect, the Catholic equivalent of the *Theologische Literaturzeitung* (No. 165), which it closely resembles. Like the *ThLZ* it opens with one or two fairly lengthy review articles. This opening section is followed by up to thirty or so double-columned pages of reviews of books, arranged under some very broad subject headings which vary slightly from issue to issue. Between thirty and forty books are looked at in any one issue. The review section is followed by a Theologische Bibliographie of about eight pages, still in double columns. This again is organized under some very general subject headings: Generalia; Biblical Studies; Church History and the History of Theology; Missiology; Religious History, Religious Studies and the Philosophy of Religion; Theology – including moral and spiritual theology – Christian Social Thought; Canon Law, Pastoral Theology, Catechetics and Liturgy. Some of the larger sections, of which the above is only an outline, are further sub-divided. There is also published annually a list of the Habilitationsschriften and doctoral dissertations presented at German, Austrian, and German-speaking Swiss universities.

COVERAGE: The scope of the *ThRv* has been sufficiently indicated by the general list of headings given above. Though the review section is limited to books, the bibliography includes periodical articles and dissertations, and helpfully analyses collections of essays. There is a strongly German bias both in the review section and in the bibliography, as well as a Catholic bias, but works and journals from all over the world find their way into *ThRv*'s pages from time to time.

COMMENT: It is somewhat difficult to judge the coverage of the *ThRv*. No list of journals scanned has been published, and the annual index limits itself to the names of the authors of reviews, or the authors of the books reviewed, or have appeared in the 'personal columns' of the journal. The review section clearly makes no claim to be exhaustive, and the German bias noticeable throughout is especially strong here. On the other hand the bibliographical section deserves to be better known. Articles are cited fairly rapidly, although books somewhat less so. The gap between publication and citation, however, is rarely more than a couple of years (the delay can be a good deal longer in the review section). The lack of a subject index, even on an annual basis, is a severe limitation on the usefulness of the *ThRv* as a tool for research purposes, and the tight layout of the page does not encourage browsing through the bibliographical section, which in any case only gives the barest details of the books and articles cited.

Published by Aschendorffsche Verlag, Sösterstrasse 13, 44
Münster, Westfalen, Federal Republic of Germany
ISSN 0040-568X

167 Theologische Zeitschrift (ThZ)

Vol. 1– ; 1945–
Six a year   24 cm

ARRANGEMENT: This is a learned journal produced by the
theological faculty of the University of Basel. Each issue
contains three or, more usually, four articles, followed by a
dozen   or   more   pages   of   book   reviews.   The
Zeitschriftenschau follows this, and normally runs to about
three pages. It is arranged by country of publication of the
journals listed.

COVERAGE: The Zeitschriftenschau interests itself in journals
which are similar in content to the *ThZ* itself, so it covers
theological and scriptural matters. As might be expected
there is a strong German-language bias, and less than half-
a-dozen English, and not many more American, journals
appear to be scanned.

COMMENT: As an additional feature for the regular readers
of *ThZ* no doubt the Zeitschriftenschau is helpful, but it is in
no way sufficiently thorough to be recommended in its own
right – though its currency is good. For the serious scholar
requiring a theological 'current awareness' service, the
Zeitschriften Inhaltsdienst Theologie (No. 177) is a much more
satisfactory tool. An additional problem is the complete lack
of any subject index, and the Zeitschriftenschau is not even
mentioned in the annual index.

Published by Friedrich Reinhardt Verlag, Missionstrasse 36,
CH-4012 Basel, Switzerland
ISSN 0040-5701

168 Unitarian Historical Society Transactions (TUHS)

Vol. 1– ; 1916–
Annual; four numbers forming a volume   21 cm

ARRANGEMENT: Each   number   (40–50   pages)   comprises

mainly historical articles or notes. There is also a section of book reviews and abstracts of periodical articles entitled Our Contemporaries. The reviews and abstracts are not arranged systematically, nor indexed.

COVERAGE: Covers Unitarian history and biography in the United Kingdom, with some reference to Presbyterian and Congregational churches and Liberal religious movements. Five or six books are reviewed annually, and about the same number of periodical articles.

COMMENT: Items are usually included within a year of publication. The reviews are a specialist guide to the literature of a robust minority, very conscious of its influence in the eighteenth and nineteenth century.

Published by the Unitarian Historical Society, 15 Giffnock Park Avenue, Glasgow G6 6AZ, Scotland, U.K.

59   United Methodist Periodical Index
Vol. 1–   ; 1961–
Quarterly; quinquennial cumulations   30 cm

ARRANGEMENT: Entries are in one alphabetical sequence, dictionary-fashion, with Library of Congress subject headings. Only minimal information necessary to trace an article is given.

COVERAGE: 68 periodicals published by the United Methodist Church are indexed, and no others. The indexing is exhaustive, taking in book reviews, short stories, poems and reproductions of works of art.

COMMENT: Many of the periodicals indexed are of a very low level, including, for example, Sunday school magazines for two- to five-year-olds. Only four scholarly journals are included in the list, all of which are indexed elsewhere. It is, therefore, of little use except for very localized studies, and there regrettably does not seem to exist a service covering Methodism in general.

Published by United Methodist Publishing House, 201
Eighth Avenue, S., Nashville, Tennessee 37202, U.S.A.
ISSN 0041-7319

170 Unpublished Writings on World Religions
Vol. 1– ; 1977–
Semi-annual   27.5 cm

ARRANGEMENT: Entries are organized under broad subject
classifications such as Religion in General, Contemporary
Religious Studies, and also by specific religious systems.
Further sub-division is, so far, unnecessary because there
have been no more than two dozen entries in each issue.
Each entry includes author, title of paper in progress or yet
to be published, pagination (including illustrative matter
and background work), the nature and status of the paper,
the major field, languages used, and date. In addition the
entries are allotted a unique number, and the number of
microfiche the entry occupies is also given.

COVERAGE: Any unpublished piece of writing on world
religious problems can be included, and the definition of
what constitutes a 'world religious problem' is a fairly wide
one. The majority of items relate to Hinduism and
Buddhism, with a few on Judaism, Comparative Religion,
and a handful on Christianity. Unpublished material is
listed, regardless of the likelihood of its eventual appearance
in print.

COMMENT: A distinctive feature of this bibliographic tool is
that items traced through it can be acquired, either in a
photocopy or on microfiche, from the Institute for the
Advanced Study of World Religions at a fairly low cost. As
the only index to work in progress and to unpublished
documents, it is of value to specialized scholars, especially
those working in the field of oriental religions.

Published by Institute for the Advanced Study of World
Religions, Melville Memorial Library, Stonybrook, New
York 11794, U.S.A.
ISSN 0149-0230

1 Verkündigung und Forschung (VF)

Vols. 1–10; 11– ; 1940–1965; 1966–

Since Volume 11 (1966) this has been a twice yearly supplement to *Evangelische Theologie*.

Semi-annual; no cumulations   23 cm

ARRANGEMENT: Each issue is a series of literature surveys. The two 1978 issues totalled 182 pages, while the individual surveys varied in length from 7 to 30 pages. Each survey (by a named contributor) begins with a detailed bibliographical list of the items surveyed and then treats the subject chronologically or by topic as appropriate. Each issue has a full index, by author, of the books and articles mentioned. There are no annual or cumulative indexes. The text is all in German.

COVERAGE: Each survey is devoted to one broad group of subjects, and six of these groups are repeated in a three- or four-year cycle. They are Old Testament, New Testament, Systematic Theology, Practical Theology, Church History and Religion/Mission/Ecumenism. Three or four more specific topics are dealt with in each issue, e.g. Christology, Introduction to Psychoanalysis, Pietism. The surveys cover books and periodical articles, and are written from a Protestant standpoint. In 1978 about 210 items were included, most of them published in German, though some were translations from other languages.

COMMENT: Where another survey had been done on the same topic in recent years, the items included were naturally fairly recent. But topics not previously covered (e.g. Old Testament themes in modern fiction) might be illustrated by items published many years before. Moreover, although the main subject fields are returned to fairly regularly, the more specific topics chosen may well be passed over for a long interval. These literature surveys appear to be mainly for a German readership and for those in a pastoral or beginning research situation. The pattern of publication makes them less suited to the systematic bibliographical search.

Published by Chr. Kaiser Verlag, Postfach 509, 800 München 43, Federal Republic of Germany
ISSN 0342-2410

172 Wesley Historical Society Proceedings

Vol. 1–   ; 1897–
Three times a year; general index to Volumes 1–30
(1897–1956)   21.5 cm

ARRANGEMENT: From 1976 an annual bibliography of Methodist historical literature has been published in each June issue, covering the period two years previous to the bibliography (e.g. the 1977 issue covers 1975). It is located in the articles section of the periodical before the book notices, and Notes and Queries. The length of the bibliography has increased each year, and in the issue examined it was nine pages. It is one complete index of authors/editors (there is no subject or title index) covering books, periodicals and thesis material. Entries give author and title (but not publisher), and in the case of books, place of publication.

COVERAGE: The subject coverage in the main is Methodist history, but it does extend to books of general nonconformist and evangelical interest, as well as the occasional non-religious books of political or economic interest. Most of the material is British, but some books are American, and some of the periodicals are from abroad – U.S.A., Norway, Germany and France. There is also a certain amount of analytical indexing in the case of Festschriften and collections of articles.

COMMENT: The bibliography suffers from not having a subject index nor, as yet, a cumulation of each year's bibliography. The decision to list all entries under an author heading, and not to use titles, leads to several articles only being listed under 'Anon', rather than the title. It provides a good general coverage and a detailed listing of specifically Methodist material, but it is not particularly up to date as a bibliography, and there are no annotations provided with the articles.

Published, c/o Editor, Rev. Dr. John C. Bowmer, 1 Matfen Place, Gosforth, Newcastle-upon-Tyne NE3 3PR, U.K.
ISSN 0043-2873

73   Women Studies Abstracts
Vol. 1– ; 1971–
Quarterly; annual index   23 cm

ARRANGEMENT: The abstracts are arranged in a classified order, one category of which is Religion. Prefatory matter includes a list of abstractors and the articles and issues covered; while the Table of Contents gives a synopsis of the classification. Each abstract has a running number, author and title, with bibliographical details, and an occasional paragraph-length abstract. (This is not really a full abstracting journal as the title might imply). The detailed index includes entries for Protestants and Ordination.

COVERAGE: The coverage is women, and some twenty or more entries per year will be of religious interest. Although there is no statement or list relating to the journals covered in the only issue consulted, coverage seems widespread and international. The journals cited for entries under Religion in the Spring 1979 issue were *USA Today*, *Bulletin of the Council on the Study of Religion*, *UNESCO Courier*, *British Medical Journal*, *Sister Advocate*, and *Christianity and Crisis*. Occasional monographs are covered.

COMMENT: The presentation is good and the index concise but useful. Despite the small number of items of direct interest to those studying religious topics, *Women Studies Abstracts* is an excellent source in its field.

Published by Rush Publishing Co., Inc., P.O. Box 1, Rush, New York 14543, U.S.A.
ISSN 0049-7835

74   Year Book of the Leo Baeck Institute
Vol. 1– ; 1955–
Annual   24 cm

ARRANGEMENT: The *Year Book* is an annual collection of

essays on the history and activities of the Jews in Germany during the past century. About a quarter of each issue, however, is devoted to Post-War Publications on German Jewry: A Selected Bibliography of Books and Articles. This appears towards the end of each book, and is followed by its own index, and the general index to the volume. Entries have been numbered consecutively year after year, nearly 16,000 items having been listed to date. The 1978 volume, published in 1979, contained nearly 2000 citations.

COVERAGE: The field covered by the bibliography is severely limited to books and articles on the history and cultural life of German-speaking Jewry – countries other than Germany itself being included. The compiler clearly ranges widely among the periodicals and books, but no list of journal titles scanned has been published. There is little of specifically religious interest included.

COMMENT: Within its strict limits this is an excellent bibliography. All entries date from the year before the *Year Book*'s publication, so currency could hardly be better. Those interested in the religious aspects of Judaism, however, will undoubtedly find *Kiryat Sefer* (No. 114) and the *Index of Articles on Jewish Studies* (No. 91) more suited to their needs.

Published by the Leo Baeck Institute, 4, Devonshire Street, London W.1, U.K.

175 **Zeitschrift für die Alttestamentliche Wissenschaft (ZAW)**
Vol. 1– ; 1881–
Three a year; cumulated indexes for Volumes 1–25 (1881–1905), 1910, and 26–50 (1906–1932), 1970   24 cm

ARRANGEMENT: Each number contains scholarly articles, reports of work in progress, Zeitschriftenschau and Bücherschau. Each volume, about 400 pages, has, among its annual indexes, an index to periodicals mentioned. The Zeitschriftenschau sections are contents lists of current periodicals arranged in alphabetical order of the periodical's title. Pagination, authors and titles of relevant articles are given with annotations, ranging from a brief expansion of the title· to a substantial abstract or brief review. The longer items are initialled. There are 64 pages in the 1975 volume. Bücherschau: these sections (62 pages in 1975) are brief reviews of monographs or Festschriften, arranged in alphabetical order of the authors' names. They are unsigned.

COVERAGE: Old Testament, its manuscripts and versions; early Judaism; ancient Middle Eastern history, culture, languages, archaeology, epigraphy, etc. Books, dissertations and periodical articles are included, mainly from the pens of Protestant scholars. About 200 books are reviewed, and articles from about 125 periodicals are noted. Items from most Western European countries and languages are reported. The reviews and annotations are in German and English. Nearly half the editorial board are based at American or British universities.

COMMENT: Most books or periodical articles were listed within twelve months of publication, and a few within six months. Others took two or three years to be listed. It is a well digested guide to recent literature for the browsing, German-reading Old Testament scholar. It is not designed for the specific subject search or for efficient scanning of particular topics over a period of years.

Published by Walter de Gruyter & Co., Genthiner Strasse 13, D-1000, Berlin 30, Federal Republic of Germany *and* 200 Saw Mill River Road, Hawthorne, New York 10532, U.S.A. ISSN 0044-2526

76 Zeitschrift für die Neutestamentliche Wissenschaft (ZNW)
und die Kunde der älteren Kirche
Vol. 1– ; 1900–
Four parts a year (usually published as 2 double numbers) 24 cm

ARRANGEMENT: This is almost entirely a journal publishing

scholarly articles in its subject field. Each issue also has a few pages of similar material entitled Miszellen and three or four pages of Zeitschriftenschau (list of current contents of periodicals). A list of books received sometimes appears. Each volume has about 300 pages. The current contents lists have no annotations. They are arranged alphabetically by the title of the periodical.

COVERAGE: New Testament, manuscripts and versions; early Christian Church, Judaic Hellenistic background; languages, archaeology, epigraphy, etc. Only a few periodical articles and book titles are listed. They are from Protestant Western European-language sources. Unlike the *ZAW* (No. 175), the *ZNW* has 90 percent German contributors.

COMMENT: The items are mostly listed within twelve months of publication. It is not really a guide to New Testament literature in the bibliographical sense. New Testament Abstracts (No. 120) and other guides should be consulted before *ZNW*.

Published by Walter de Gruyter & Co., Genthiner Strasse 13, D-1000, Berlin 30, Federal Republic of Germany *and* 200 Saw Mill River Road, Hawthorne, New York 10532, U.S.A. ISSN 0084-5329

177 Zeitschriften Inhaltdienst Theologie (ZIT)
Indices theologici
Vol. 1– ; 1976–
Monthly; annual indexes   21 cm

ARRANGEMENT: Each issue contains reproductions of the contents pages of a variety of journals covering religion and theology. These are organized into eleven major subject areas, each of which is given a code letter of some mnemonic value (B = Bibelwissenschaft, KR = Kirchenrecht). These letters, however, give no clue to the order in which the sections appear. There is an additional section (F) for Festschriften and Sammelwerke. Within each section the entries are arranged alphabetically by journal title, and they are supplemented by three indexes: personal name, Biblical quotation and author.

COVERAGE: *ZIT* is limited to the 350 or so periodicals in the fields of Bible studies, Church history, dogmatics, Canon Law, Ecumenics, Missions, Orthodox Churches and Religious Studies taken by the university library at Tübingen. This degree of 'limitation' is scarcely a problem, however, for the vast majority of these are 'core' periodicals, though there is a natural bias towards German-language ones. This bias, such as it is, has the advantage of drawing attention to some lesser-known journals in German. Abour 160 journal parts are included in each issue, suggesting a minimum of some 800 articles indexed each month.

COMMENT: Apart from the Birmingham Public Library's *Guide to Religious Periodical Literature* (No. 87) *ZIT* appears to be the only 'current awareness' service in the field of religion and theology. It has the customary drawback of this type of publication, in that there are no abstracts to indicate the true nature (or value) of the articles mentioned, and articles without a descriptive title constitute a greater problem. On the other hand, *ZIT*'s clarity of presentation and speed of production (a maximum of twelve weeks between the publication of a journal and its listing) more than compensate for this. The computer-produced indexes, and particularly the annual ones, add considerably to the value of *ZIT*, which can be used both for current and for retrospective searching.

Published by Universitätsbibliothek, Tübingen, Federal Republic of Germany
ISSN 0340-8361

78 Zwingliana (Zwing.)
Beiträge zur Geschichte Zwinglis der Reformation und des Protestantismus in der Schweiz
Vol. 1– ; 1897–
Semi-annual; quinquennial index   23 cm

ARRANGEMENT: Each issue (of 60–70 pages) has one or two

scholarly articles and some short book reviews; alternate issues have a bibliographical section as well. The latter (5–10 pages) has recently been devoted to literature on the history of the Reformation in Switzerland, and arranged in four sections: bibliography, collective studies, editions of original texts, and individual studies (each section arranged alphabetically by author or editor). There are brief annotations in German or English. This section is not cumulated or indexed, though each issue of it is noted in the quinquennial volume's contents lists. The books in each book review section (5–10 pages) are listed individually in the quinquennial index.

COVERAGE: Life and work of Huldreich Zwingli (1484–1531) and other Swiss Reformers (e.g. Heinrich Bullinger); relationship with Calvin, Luther and other reformers; with Erasmus and humanism; and with other reform movements, e.g. Anabaptists, Mennonites. Books, dissertations and periodical articles are listed. Selection is naturally from a Protestant viewpoint. About 100 entries a year are included. The periodicals covered are few, but the range of languages and sources covers Western Europe and U.S.A.

COMMENT: All items are included within two years of publication, some within six months. But note current delay of twelve months in distribution. Most libraries would find the Literaturbericht of the *Archiv für Reformationsgeschichte* (No. 24) sufficiently inclusive for recent material on this period, but for the Swiss Reformation and for Zwingli in particular this specialist index would be complementary.

Published for the Zwingliverein at the Zentralbibliothek, Zürich, by Verlag Berichthaus Zürich, Zwingliplatz 3, 8022 Zürich 1, Switzerland

Indexes

Subject Index

References relate to the entry numbers given to the publications in this *Guide*.

Subject index

Humanities, Asia, 42, 86
Hymnology, 107
see also Liturgy

Iconography, 40, 62, 63
India, 42, 61, 86
Interfaith Relationships, 102, 104,
  110, 119, 122
see also Ecumenical Affairs
Intertestamental Literature, *see*
  Old Testament
Ireland, History, 14, 18, 46, 116
Islam, 3, 47, 61, 117, 119, 132, 135,
  154A
Islam, Philosophy, 127
Israel, State of, 114
see also Judaism

Jesuits (Society of Jesus), 29
see also Religious Orders
Jewish Studies, *see* Judaism
Jews, Germany, 174
Judaism, 47, 61, 91, 112, 114, 117,
  156
Judaism, History, 48, 101, 108,
  154A, 175
see also Biblical Studies

Latin Studies, 13, 154A
see also Christianity, Early
  History; Medieval Studies;
  Patristics; Roman Studies
Liturgy, 23, 30, 36, 83, 101, 107,
  133, 154
see also Byzantine Studies;
  Catechesis
Low Countries, Church History, 19
Luther and the Lutheran Church,
  115
see also Reformation

Magic (Primitive Religion), 98, 99
Medical Ethics, 1, 43
see also Bioethics; Ethics
Medieval Studies, 13, 57, 59, 68,
  101, 116, 118, 135, 142, 155
see also Patristics
Methodist Church, 169, 172

Middle East, *see* Near East
Ministry, 99, 102
see also Mission and Missions;
  Pastoral Work
Mission and Missions, 2, 32, 60,
  102, 113, 171
Mission, Urban, 2, 113
Monasticism, 59
see also Cistercian Order;
  Religious Orders; Spirituality
Moral Philosophy, *see* Ethics
Mormonism, 93
Muslim Studies, *see* Islam
Mysticism, *see* Spirituality
Myth and Mythology, 40, 98, 99
see also Primitive Religion

Near East, 47, 55, 114, 117, 119, 132
Near East, History, 48, 82, 101, 105,
  108, 124, 154A, 156, 175, 176
see also Biblical Studies;
  Christianity, Early History;
  Islam
Netherlands, Church History, 19
New Testament, 120, 121, 171, 176
see also Biblical Studies;
  Christianity, Early History
Nonconformists, Eastern Europe,
  136
Nonconformists, France, 56
Nonconformists, Great Britain, 58,
  172
North Africa, Islam, 132

Old Testament, 48, 91, 123, 124,
  171, 175
see also Biblical Studies; Judaism;
  Near East, History
Order of Friars Minor
  (Franciscans), 6, 28, 34
Orthodox Church, 106, 125, 136
see also Byzantine Studies;
  Church History

Papacy, The, 30, 59, 128
Pastoral Work, 102, 126
see also Ministry; Mission and
  Missions

Title Index

This index lists the titles of publications mentioned in this *Guide.* It includes not only the principal titles used to arrange the entries in the *Guide*, but also superseded titles, alternative titles, titles of parent publications and the titles of supplementary bibliographical sections. References relate to entry numbers.

Title index

211